PYGMALION

Shaw's Spin on Myth and Cinderella

TWAYNE'S MASTERWORK STUDIES

Robert Lecker, General Editor

PYGMALION

Shaw's Spin on Myth and Cinderella

Charles A. Berst

TWAYNE PUBLISHERS
An Imprint of Simon & Schuster Macmillan
New York

Prentice Hall International
London   Mexico City   New Delhi   Singapore   Sydney   Toronto

Twayne's Masterwork Series No. 155

Pygmalion: *Shaw's Spin on Myth and Cinderella*
Charles A. Berst

Twayne Publishers
An Imprint of Simon & Schuster Macmillan
866 Third Avenue
New York, New York 10022

Library of Congress Cataloging-in-Publication Data

Berst, Charles A.
    Pygmalion : Shaw's play with myth and Cinderella / Charles A. Berst.
        p.   cm. — (Masterwork studies; 155)
    Includes bibliographical references and index.
    ISBN 0-8057-9447-6 — ISBN 0-8057-4538-6 (pbk.)
    Shaw, Bernard, 1865–1950. Pygmalion. 2. Cinderella (Legendary character) in literature. 3. Mythology in literature. 4. Folklore in literature. I. Title. II. Series: Twayne's masterwork studies; no. 155.
PR5363.P83B47   1995
822'.912—dc20   95-1980
                                                                                                      CIP

The paper used in this publication meets the minimum requirements of American National Standard for Information Sciences—Permanence of Paper for Printed Library Materials. ANSI Z3948–1984.∞™

10 9 8 7 6 5 4 3 2 1 (hc)
10 9 8 7 6 5 4 3 2 1 (pb)

Printed in the United States of America

Contents

George Bernard Shaw at 63. Portrait by Elliott and Fry, 1919.

Note on *Pygmalion's* Text and Style and Acknowledgments

The edition of *Pygmalion* that this book will follow is the "definitive" one currently published by Penguin Books (London and New York). Page numbers in parentheses in the following discussion refer to that edition. Since the play will be addressed chronologically, these page citations will be periodic, to enable the reader to find contexts easily.

There will be occasional references to earlier editions. The first edition, published with *Androcles and the Lion* and *Overruled* in 1916 (London: Constable and Company), included Shaw's prose addition at the end of the play. Shaw's script for the 1938 English film has been published in *The Collected Screen Plays of Bernard Shaw*, edited by Bernard F. Dukore (Athens: University of Georgia Press, 1980). The current edition used here reflects Penguin's 1941 paperback, which included film scenes Shaw adapted especially for it, a new ending to act 5 that was first published in a 1939 reprint from the Standard Edition of his works (Constable), revisions he also made to the preface and to the end of act 4, and drawings by Feliks Topolski.

In the "Note for Technicians" preceding the play, Shaw comments that "for ordinary theatrical use the scenes separated by rows of asterisks [selected film scenes] are to be omitted." Since they become part of the reader's experience, however, and since some of them may occasionally be staged, we will examine their qualities in relation to the rest, trying to maintain a double sense of the play, that is, both without and with these scenes. Like Shaw's revisions, they offer interesting choices.

Shaw's spelling and punctuation were often idiosyncratic. He sought economy in both. Happily for us, he favored American spelling (*color* for *colour*, *humor* for *humour*), but occasionally he could be independent or archaic (as with *Shakespear* or *shew*). Similarly, he often omitted apostrophes where he thought them superfluous (hence, *dont* or *weve*, but *he'll* or *I'll*). These are reproduced according to his instincts. Words in which he spaced letters to indicate emphasis have been changed to italics.

My grateful thanks to Robert Lecker, the general editor of this series, and to Mark Zadrozny, Twayne's editor, for their consistent patience and care, and to Cindy Buck for her very accomplished and thorough copyediting. To my wife Roelina I am deeply indebted for enduring inspiration, understanding, and the beauties of life. And in such delights my daughters Caroline and Nelina, and son-in-law Clifford, are one with her.

Chronology: George Bernard Shaw's Life and Works

1856   George Bernard Shaw born on 26 July in a small Dublin row house, the third child and only son of George Carr Shaw, an unsuccessful grain merchant, and Lucinda Elizabeth Gurly, daughter of a money-strapped country gentleman.

1859   Darwin's *Origin of Species* provokes much debate.

1860–1866   Father's alcoholism, mother's scant affection, and family's snobbishness, despite its poverty, give Shaw "the devil of a childhood." Tutored a bit, but learns most from visits to Dublin's slums, the family's delight in music, and precocious reading, including Shakespeare, Dickens, Bunyan, *The Arabian Nights*, and the Bible.

1866–1868   Mother's voice teacher, a musical entrepreneur named Vandeleur Lee, joins the family. The Shaws and Lee move to Lee's sea-view cottage, then to his larger house in Dublin.

1867   Publication of Marx's *Das Kapital*, written in the Reading Room of the British Museum.

1867–1871   Dislikes his spotty schooling and (Protestant) church. Mostly educated through further reading, the household's immersion in music under Lee, and haunting the National Gallery, operas, and plays.

1871   Becomes a clerk in an estate agent's office.

1872   His mother takes his sisters and follows Lee to London, to teach singing.

1876   Leaves his clerkship to join his mother: "I did not throw myself into the struggle for life, I threw my mother into it." One sister dies, the other becomes a professional singer.

	Ghostwrites music criticism and essays for Lee, whose career and repute with the family decline.
1878	Starts but abandons a cynical "passion play" in blank verse.
1879	Joins the Zetetical ("truth-seeking") Society and meets Sidney Webb. Completes first novel, with a semiautobiographical hero, and titles it *Immaturity*.
1880	Quits a job with the Edison Telephone Company and completes second novel, about a consummate rationalist. Starts years of self-education in the British Museum's Reading Room. Joins socialist, debating, and literary societies. Starts a formidable speaking career. Considers himself an outsider.
1881	Following Shelley's example, becomes a vegetarian. After a long bout with smallpox, grows his famous beard, rapidly assuming a diabolical image.
1881–1883	Writes three more novels. Their heroes—a composer, a prizefighter, a socialist—embody his interests. None succeeds commercially, yet upon reading one, Robert Louis Stevenson exclaims, "My God . . . what women!"
1882	Begins a tempestuous three-year love affair with Alice Lockett.
1882–1883	A lecture by Henry George, *Das Kapital*, and Shaw's studies make him a lifelong socialist: "Marx made a man of me."
1884	Joins the (socialist) Fabian Society and brings Sidney Webb into it. They soon take leading roles.
1885	Starts but abandons his first full-length play. Earns small sums through journalism: "Better see rightly on a pound a week than squint on a million." Loses his virginity to an aggressive widow, Jenny Patterson.
1886–1889	Art critic for *The World*. Gains renown as a public speaker.
1887	Edits *Fabian Essays*, contributing two.
1888–1890	Irreverent music critic for *The Star*, using a playful pseudonym, Corno di Bassetto: "It was as Punch, then, that I emerged from obscurity."
1890–1894	Music reviews for *The World* as "G.B.S." make him one of the greatest music critics of all time. A journalist remarks, "Everybody in London knows Shaw," and amorous women pursue him. His correspondence burgeons toward the estimated 250,000 letters he will write during his lifetime.
1891	Writes *The Quintessence of Ibsenism*, becoming the foremost English champion of Henrik Ibsen's plays.

Chronology

1892	*Widowers' Houses*, his first play, is performed just twice but attracts notoriety: "I had not achieved success; but I had provoked an uproar; and the sensation was so agreeable that I resolved to try again."
1893	Writes his second and third plays, *The Philanderer* and *Mrs. Warren's Profession*. The first is not produced; the second, dealing with prostitution, is banned by the censor.
1894	Turns from "unpleasant" social dramas to "pleasant" plays: *Arms and the Man* (a minor success that does not profit financially) and *Candida*.
1895	Writes *You Never Can Tell* and *The Man of Destiny*. Neither is produced. Starts famous tenure as drama critic for the *Saturday Review*.
1896	Affectionate correspondence with renowned actress Ellen Terry gains steam. Oscar Wilde imprisoned for homosexuality. Writes *The Devil's Disciple*.
1897	*The Devil's Disciple* triumphs in America, bringing in his first substantial income. Serves as vestryman, then as councillor for the London borough of St. Pancras until 1903.
1898	Publishes his early plays. Debilitated by overwork and a foot infection, resigns as drama critic, discontinues frequent lecturing, and marries an "Irish millionairess," Charlotte Payne-Townshend. During honeymoon-recuperation, completes *Caesar and Cleopatra* and *The Perfect Wagnerite* (about Wagner's *Ring*).
1899	Writes *Captain Brassbound's Conversion*.
1901	Queen Victoria dies. Starts *Man and Superman*.
1903	Publishes *Man and Superman*. H. G. Wells joins the Fabians.
1904–1907	The Royal Court Theatre, with Harley Granville Barker and J. E. Vedrenne as managers, features his plays each season. Writes *John Bull's Other Island*, *Major Barbara*, *The Doctor's Dilemma*, and shorter plays while continuing Fabian activities. Popularity assured when portly King Edward VII laughs so hard at *John Bull's Other Island* that his chair breaks.
1908–1911	Continued success with *Getting Married*, *Misalliance*, and *Fanny's First Play*. Retires from the Fabian Executive Committee.
1912	Writes *Androcles and the Lion* and *Pygmalion*. Falls in love with Mrs. Patrick Campbell.

1913	Mother dies. Mrs. Patrick Campbell jilts him. *Pygmalion* premieres in Vienna.
1914	*Pygmalion* triumphs in London. World War I begins. Writes *Common Sense About the War*, which blames all sides and raises a storm of jingoistic outrage.
1915–1916	Responds to the war's ferment. Writes incidental playlets.
1917	Tours the western front as respect for his views on the war increases. Completes *Heartbreak House*. Revolution in Russia.
1918–1919	The war ends. Women enfranchised. Starts *Back to Methuselah*.
1920	Sister Lucy dies. Completes *Back to Methuselah*. New York Theatre Guild premieres *Heartbreak House*. League of Nations formed.
1921	Irish Free State established.
1922	Theatre Guild premieres *Back to Methuselah*. Mrs. Patrick Campbell tries to publish his love letters to her, but he edits them and starts playing Henry Higgins to Molly Tompkins, a young American would-be actress.
1923	Writes *Saint Joan*, which attracts worldwide acclaim. W. B. Yeats receives Nobel Prize in Literature.
1924	First Labour government elected. With a bushy white beard, Shaw now looks more like a deity than a devil. He and his wife virtually adopt T. E. Lawrence (Lawrence of Arabia).
1925	Awarded Nobel Prize in Literature. Peak of international fame; often cited as "news" in the *New York Times*.
1926–1927	Receives tributes from Einstein, Mann, Spengler, Richard Strauss. Labors on *The Intelligent Woman's Guide to Socialism and Capitalism*. Philanders with Molly Tompkins in Italy.
1929	Submits *The Apple Cart* for the Malvern Festival, which features his plays until 1940. Churchill praises continuing relevance of *Major Barbara*.
1930	First novel is at last published, in the Standard Edition of his works.
1931	Writes *Too True to be Good*. Visits the Soviet Union with Lady Nancy Astor; talks with Stalin; praises Soviet government.
1932	Visits South Africa, where he writes *The Adventures of the Black Girl in Her Search for God*. Starts a world cruise.
1933	Acclaimed on visits to India, China, Japan, Hollywood, New York. Writes *On the Rocks* and *Village Wooing*.

Chronology

1934   Visits New Zealand. Writes *The Simpleton of the Unexpected Isles* and *The Millionairess*. Hitler consolidates Nazi power.

1935   Agrees to have Gabriel Pascal film some of his plays.

1936   King George V dies; Edward VIII abdicates. Writes *Geneva*, including Hitler, Mussolini, and Franco as characters.

1937   Hitler-Mussolini alliance.

1938   Film of *Pygmalion* breaks box-office records; Shaw receives an Academy Award for the screenplay.

1939   Completes *In Good King Charles's Golden Days*. World War II begins.

1940   *Major Barbara* filmed. Mrs. Patrick Campbell dies.

1943   Wife Charlotte dies at 86. Completes *Everybody's Political What's What*.

1945   World War II ends when Germany surrenders in May and United States drops atomic bomb on Japan in August. *Caesar and Cleopatra* filmed.

1946   Addresses the public in a radio broadcast celebrating his ninetieth birthday. Granville Barker and H. G. Wells die.

1947   Completes *Buoyant Billions*. Sidney Webb dies.

1949   Publishes *Sixteen Self Sketches*. Writes *Shakes versus Shav* (Shakespeare versus Shaw) for puppets:

> Tomorrow and tomorrow and tomorrow
>
> We puppets shall replay our scene.

1950   On 10 September breaks hip while pruning trees. Dies 2 November. His will supports the creation of a phonetic alphabet.

HISTORICAL AND
LITERARY CONTEXT

1

The Interplay of History, Life, and Myth

Eliza Doolittle was born in the mid-1890s, years that capped a revolutionary century. England had led the modern world in evolving from a primarily agrarian, rural, aristocratic society into an industrial, urban, democratic one. As the world's first industrial country, it had become the world's banker and greatest trading nation. Avoiding the tumultuous political upheavals that had disrupted the Continent, it capitalized on stability with peaceful revolutions in politics, economics, and science.

These successes had produced profound social changes. In 1832 a Reform Bill had given middle classes the vote and transferred political power from the countryside to cities. Then in 1867 a second Reform Bill gave workingmen the vote, leading to broad-based democracy and stimulating socialist activities, which that same year found a secular bible in Marx's *Das Kapital*. Meanwhile, Darwin's *Origin of Species* (1859) and *Descent of Man* (1870) convinced many not only that humans had evolved less in God's image than from ancient sea slime, but also that survival of the fittest was nature's gospel. And if this new gospel was so, then survival of the fittest under capitalism naturally suited an evolving society. England's burgeoning middle class, so full of energy, morality, and ideals, proved its merit.

Or did it? Bernard Shaw was among those who challenged England's self-satisfaction. Could the country and its expanding middle classes be proud when, despite reforms, England was rife with social inequities and urban poverty? The Covent Garden scene that opens *Pygmalion* draws implicit social lines: the "squashed cabbage leaf" poor, the lower-middle class, a family clinging to gentility, and the genteel middle class—embodied, respectively, in Eliza, a crowd, the Eynsford Hills, and Henry Higgins and Colonel Pickering.

Shaw was intimately acquainted with the lower end of this spectrum. Many critics have compared him with Higgins, yet his origins were closer to Eliza's. He was born in Dublin in a cramped row house and, much as Eliza might have, called his beginnings "the devil of a childhood." His family thought itself thoroughly middle- or upper-middle-class yet lived in "genteel poverty" (like the Eynsford Hills), a "ridiculous poverty" fraught with pretensions he deplored. His Protestant parents felt superior to Ireland's Catholics yet seldom attended church. His father, a covert alcoholic and poor businessman, was a middle-class Alfred Doolittle who did little and laughed at his own failure. Mrs. Shaw (called Bessie, a variant of Elizabeth or Eliza) gave affection to her two daughters but little to her son. Like Eliza, he was forced to be independent, and visits to Dublin's slums showed him squalidness that would have been familiar to her.

Shaw's schooling was better than Eliza's, but he found it wretched and mostly educated himself through voracious reading, visiting the National Gallery, escaping to the countryside, attending dramas and operas, and experiencing music rehearsals that his mother's voice teacher, George Vandeleur Lee, brought into the house. The remote possibility that Lee was his father could account for the many illegitimate offspring (such as Eliza) in his plays. In any event, Shaw's life turned especially bleak when his mother took his sisters and followed Lee to London, leaving him at 15 (much as Eliza is left) to make his way in a grubby world. As Eliza peddles flowers, Shaw clerked for four years. As she has dreams and ambitions, so did he. No Higgins threw him change, but like Eliza he finally realized that he was at a dead end, whereupon he followed his mother to London and lived penuriously off her income as a voice teacher. Eliza seeks education on her own. So did Shaw. In London he joined literary, cultural, and debating societies and overcame shyness and ineptitude by forcing himself to articulate his ideas (as Eliza learns to). Soon he made the Reading Room of the British Museum his substitute for college.

Before long, he underwent a metamorphosis as striking as Eliza's, and far more bizarre. While her transformation echoes the myths of Pygmalion and Cinderella, Shaw's was perversely biblical: he grew a roughly pointed reddish beard and, on the advice of a voice teacher (a Swiss precursor of Higgins), combed his hair into two peaks atop his forehead. Voilà! The studious introvert assumed a devilish mien. Much as Eliza's transformation springs from her education and increased self-confidence, so did Shaw's. Yet while hers evokes middle-class romance, his led him to puncture middle-class assumptions. She becomes a lady; he became a socialist. After Eliza uses her training to attack Higgins near the end of *Pygmalion*, the professor exclaims, "By George, Eliza, I said I'd make a woman of you." After Shaw read *Das Kapital*, he attacked Marx's economics but declared: "Marx made a man of me." To succeed, Eliza uses acting talents and wit; so did Shaw. Yet beneath these talents and their comic elements she has a very serious side, and so did he.[1]

Higgins-like aspects in Shaw appeared, appropriately enough, when he turned to socialism, assumed his diabolical likeness, and became first a critic of society, music, and theater, and finally a playwright who combined all of these interests. Thus, the heroine and hero of *Pygmalion* not only embody two aspects of their author's life but pit his youth against elements of his middle age. At the same time, the author's experience and social views inform the play, and the play in turn transmutes these into something permanent and sublime.

Shaw manages all this most artfully by having Eliza's evolution echo famous fantasies: the metamorphoses of "Pygmalion" and "Cinderella," with touches of the devil and Eve complementing both. To appreciate the magic of this artistry, we should recall the myth and fairy tale.

The Pygmalion Myth

The major source of the Pygmalion myth is an episode in Ovid's *Metamorphoses*, written in Rome shortly after the year 1 A.D. Adapting ancient legends, Ovid starts with a brief account of women on Cyprus who denied the divinity of Venus and became, through her wrath, the first prostitutes, whereupon they lost their shame and hardened into flint. Disgusted by such female corruption, Pygmalion languishes unmarried. Yet celibacy has its limits, so with marvelous artistry he sculpts an ivory statue of a girl more perfect, more beautiful, than any ever born—and falls in love with his creation. His art conceals itself so ingeniously that the statue seems alive, as though it desires to *move*, were it not deterred by modesty. Afire with passion for this image, hardly believing it only ivory, Pygmalion caresses it, imagines his kisses returned, speaks to it, embraces it, fears to bruise it, and brings it little gifts that girls enjoy. He decks it with robes, rings, necklaces, and earrings but finds it no less beautiful naked, and he lays it on a couch, softly cushioning its head, calling it his bedfellow, his darling.

At the time of Cyprus's grand festival for Venus, Pygmalion timidly prays that he might have as a wife—he dares not say "my ivory girl"—"one *like* my ivory girl." Venus understands; three times the altar flames leap high. Returning home, Pygmalion leans over his beloved and kisses her: she seems *warm*. Putting his lips to hers again, he strokes her breast and the ivory grows soft. Amazed, rejoicing, doubting, he strokes again and again: her veins throb as he presses them—she has a human body! He pours forth thanks to Venus. Feeling his kisses, the girl blushes and timidly lifts her eyes to the light and her lover. After nine full moons, their daughter is born.[2]

Cinderella

Cinderella motifs have surfaced throughout the world. One Chinese version is over 1,000 years old, and more than 500 variants have appeared in Europe. These often include a cruel stepmother, the girl's dead mother (or a bird or animal agent of the mother), who provides rich clothing for the ball, and a prince who identifies his sweetheart by means of a golden or silver slipper or a shoe, ring, spindle, or thread.

The tale's most popular version comes from Charles Perrault, an elderly Frenchman whose "Cendrillon" was published in 1697 in a collection that soon became known as *Tales of Mother Goose*. Features that distinguish the tale for most of us are largely his: the fairy godmother; the transformation of a pumpkin, mice, a rat, and lizards into a coach, horses, a coachman, and footmen; the midnight deadline; and the slipper made of glass. Delightful as these are, equally engaging is Perrault's orchestration of them. His story moves nimbly, with rich accretions of imagination often grounded in touches of logic. His godmother, for example, appears in a motherly fashion because Cinderella is distressed, and the godmother's magic has not only charm but a metaphoric rationale: a pumpkin with wheels resembles a golden coach, lithe mice make ideal horses, a fat rat with whiskers makes a coachman, lizards with their tails resemble footmen in livery. The clock striking twelve visits a deadline on the timelessness of romance. It makes time sensory, tolls a shift to stark realities, and marks a curfew for children. The glass slippers contrast with the cinders Cinderella is escaping. Their fragility reflects her status, their transparency evokes her purity in a subtly erotic way, and her comfort in their glistening uniqueness makes their romance exotic and fitting.

Perrault also grounds his fancy in very human characters and touches. The stepmother is not simply evil, as in other versions, but proud, haughty, and a bit to be pitied: "She could not bear the good qualities of the young girl, for they made her own daughters seem even less likeable." When Cinderella weeps after her stepsisters leave for the ball, her godmother appears not supernaturally but as familiarly as Aunt Biddy from the next room, and when Cinderella sputters like a little girl ("If only I could . . . if only I could . . ."), the godmother responds just like an old Biddy: "Well, be a good girl and I'll get you there." The coach, horses, coachman, footmen, and resplendent dress materialize, like the godmother, from household particulars that she and the girl gather like children at play; whereupon Biddy, like a prudent parent, warns her innocent, romantic charge not to linger after midnight, when charms give way to realities.

Perrault makes Cinderella's growth from a girl to a woman more important than the hocus-pocus of her transformation. When she appears as a princess at the ball, all stand fascinated by her beauty. The king, "old as he was, could not take his eyes off her," and the ladies note her clothes and hair, hoping to imitate her. For them, appearance is virtually enough. But after all, a princess is as a princess does—and Cinderella meets this test too. After dancing with the prince, she combines the graciousness of a lady with the gifts of a child by sitting next to her stepsisters, "offering them oranges and lemons which the Prince had given her," and chatting with them until quarter to twelve. After her return to homely realities, Cinderella's maturity grows according to her new situation, and when the slipper fits and she marries the prince, she promptly forgives her sisters. Two morals follow the tale. The first concludes: "To capture a heart, beyond question to win it,/Graciousness is the gift with true magic in it." More realistically, the second finds that more is needed: "To succeed as you should" (assuming you should), "you need godmothers, too."[3]

Shaw's echoing of such themes gives *Pygmalion* fanciful delights and mythical force.

2

A Masterwork?

How can so portentous a term as "masterwork" apply to a romantic comedy? Many aspects of *Pygmalion* prove its case. Here are some of the important ones.

HISTORICAL ASPECTS

As a twentieth-century theatrical phenomenon, *Pygmalion* is distinctive in at least three ways. First, it is a major play by an author whose dramatic canon is both so large and of such high quality that many consider him the greatest English playwright after Shakespeare. Second, it is one of at least a dozen of his plays that continue to meet the test of time as living theater, appearing again and again in professional revivals. Third, it has proved immensely popular and durable in three versions: as a play, whose first English production was a sensation in 1914; as a film, which won international praise and an Academy Award in 1938; and as the source of an even more famous musical of the late 1950s, *My Fair Lady*, which became an equally successful film. No other modern play has matched its distinction across these three mediums.

The play's durability as living theater is especially important. Some academic critics underplay the fact that dramas involve performance. Plays by Byron and Shelley and Browning, however good they may be as literature, are now deader than doornails: unperformed, they have fallen short of dramatic point. A 75-year (or three-generation) test may be fair. How many English dramas written between 1800 and 1920 continue to receive professional performances? Against Shaw's dozen or more and several by Oscar Wilde, fewer than six by all other playwrights combined.

Artistic Aspects

Of course, durability alone does not assure quality. To assess *Pygmalion* as a masterwork, one must engage drama's distinctive elements. In contrast to novels and poetry, the theater involves physical action, settings, sound, lighting, interpretation through directors and actors, and a collective audience. A playwright must consider all of these elements, which provide many aesthetic opportunities but also have limits that novels do not, such as less flexibility in changes of locale, fewer imaginative panoramas, and usually fewer characters, whose roles rely on the talents of actors. Then, too, a playwright must show more than tell, a particular problem in representing characters who have thoughts apart from what they say. Limited time may be most constraining of all. No matter how complex the story and its characters and background, it must be conveyed in a few hours. This restriction compels an artistic economy closer to poetry than to novels—poetry involving special effects as it unfolds on a stage. As in poetry, metaphors and the interrelation of metaphors often become crucial tools of economy and aesthetics.

In fine dramas, these elements also make special demands on critics. Since this study will engage such demands, it may be well to answer Wordsworth's "The Tables Turned," in which a speaker derides "meddling intellect," declaring that "we murder to dissect."

Defying this view, the following pages will dissect and dissect. As a socialist, Shaw dissected society; as a critic, he dissected the performances of actors and musicians; as a playwright, he dissected characters and revised scenes. His purpose was seldom to murder but rather to perceive individuals, societies, events, and ideas as clearly as possible, and thus to present them to audiences with distinctive sharpness and force. In almost any art, dissection is a part of the creative process; in criticism, it can be immensely revealing. If an artwork is weak, dissecting can indeed murder it (it may deserve murdering). If it is strong, however, dissecting discovers the vitality of its components, often unleashing compounds of life within life within life, which in turn interrelate with the life of other components. Thus, dissection can illuminate the vital powers of fine art.

This, as we shall see, is the case with *Pygmalion*, in which Shaw exploits the potentials of drama through varied and vital dramatic poetry.

A DIDACTIC ASPECT

Contrary to many who believe that teaching has no place in art, Shaw declares in his preface to *Pygmalion* that the play is "intensely and deliberately didactic. . . . It goes to prove my contention that great art can never be anything else" (9). His subject at hand is phonetics, yet elsewhere he explains that all great art is didactic in the profound sense that it refines and expands one's consciousness.[1] Insofar as Eliza's increasing self-realization and other factors in the play stimulate our perceptions and awareness of phonetics, social distinctions, and life, we and they exemplify Shaw's point.

ROMANTIC ASPECTS

Will Higgins marry Eliza? Should Higgins marry Eliza? What about Eliza and lovestruck Freddy? Deeper yet, what about the sheer romance of a flower girl who transcends social barriers to become an impressive lady? Such questions become tests of our sensibilities as well as of the play.

REALISTIC ASPECTS

Girding *Pygmalion*'s romance, the characters attract us by their accessible, sharply defined humanity, and their individuality is etched both logically and memorably by dramatic contexts and settings. For all his oddity, even Doolittle passes muster as a trash collector in the vein of philosophic down-and-outers.

SOCIAL ASPECTS

The status and interaction of the play's characters make telling social points. If language and dress and manners can pass a flower girl off as a lady, what distinguishes a lady? How valid is social status based less on one's merit than on one's family and money? How many wrongs should a birthright right if a birthright could right wrongs?

AUTOBIOGRAPHICAL ASPECTS

We have glanced at the vitality of these in the previous chapter. Normally, such aspects should be peripheral to an artwork, but when an author is as famous a "character" as Shaw, a work like *Pygmalion* may be charged with extra vibrations from life.

MYTHICAL ASPECTS

These complement *Pygmalion*'s realism with archetypal metaphors. Walt Disney recognized the (cash) value of the most popular one Shaw uses when he wrote Charles Koerner of Paramount Studios in 1944:

"CINDERELLA, to us, is a very important property. . . . The name CINDERELLA has a special significance . . . in the public's mind, insofar as it concerns a special type of story and character. There seems to be a new interest in the Cinderella-type of story—for example, 'CINDERELLA SWINGS IT,' 'CINDERELLA JONES,' and so on. If this continues I feel it will depreciate the value of the original CINDERELLA story. I would, therefore, appreciate any consideration on your part to help me protect the title of this property."[2]

Why not copyright Santa Claus? Disney's "important property," "depreciate the value of," "appreciate," "consideration," and "protect the title of this property" sound less like the guru of a Magic Kingdom than a speculator in California real estate. Still, *Cinderella* (1950) bounced Disney's studio out of the doldrums and financed Disneyland, which might well have been dubbed Cinderellaland.

More subtly than Disney yet equally appreciating the powers of myth, Shaw houses "Pygmalion," "Cinderella," and the devil under the title *Pygmalion* to point up Eliza's creation from a male sculptor's viewpoint, even though he knew that "Cinderella," involving creation from a girl's viewpoint, would have been a more familiar title. Higgins clearly lacks the eroticism of Ovid's Pygmalion, but his distaste for women in life's gutters, his passion for creation, for an art that conceals its art in carving a thing of beauty from raw materials, his dressing Eliza in gowns and jewels, and his desire to articulate life and achieve an ideal, all echo Ovid's hero. Pygmalion's passions finally impregnate his creation; Higgins's finally spark Eliza to give birth to the woman within her.

The popular imagination, which downplays Cinderella's character and growth nearly as much as Perrault plays them up, may even stir her with Pygmalion into a common romantic soufflé: to wit, aided by benevolent hocus-pocus, lovelorn Pygmalion creates an ideal woman and weds her, and lovelorn Cinderella leaves persecution to wed an ideal prince. This reductive fluff not only neglects the artistry that gives both tales depth but blurs the differences that distinguish them. Each version has ambiguity and subtlety. Ovid's sculptor creates an image of ideal womanhood, but Venus, not he, gives his dream life.

Perrault's heroine seeks liberation, a quest in which her virtue and graciousness are more important than a prince.

Ultimately, for all the powers of Pygmalion and Cinderella as ancient archetypes, their most enduring form derives from Ovid's and Perrault's distinctive renditions, and Shaw's updated combination of the two seems similarly on its way to a major place in the mythic tradition.

SPIRITUAL ASPECTS

Beyond the echoes of Pygmalion and Cinderella, Shaw's depiction of Eliza's growth and of the diabolical qualities in Higgins that spur and challenge it evokes not only humor but a serious aspect as well. Her growth, after all, involves increasing self-realization, an evolution from a lower to a higher state of being, and as such it has spiritual qualities that give strength and resonance to the play's fun.

Shaw once referred to *Pygmalion* as a potboiler. At a certain level of genius, it seems, pots boil deeply. Finally, the play is a masterwork not just in the multiplicity of its aspects but in the superlative art with which it displays, explores, and interrelates all its aspects with humor, depth, and seeming ease.

3

Brouhaha and Critics

Much as *Pygmalion*'s Cinderella motif has helped its popularity soar, the play's popularity has spurred the attention of critics, ranging from many who address its sources, themes, and aesthetics to others who relate it to biographical and psychological aspects of its author.

The critical view most readers encounter first is Shaw's. His preface delivers a jolt. Ignoring comedy and romance, it highlights a rarefied subject: "The English have no respect for their language, and will not teach their children to speak it. . . . The reformer we need most today is an energetic phonetic enthusiast: that is why I have made such a one the hero of a popular play . . . if the play makes the public aware that there are such people as phoneticians, and that they are among the most important people in England at present, it will serve its turn" (5, 9). For an example, he reminisces about his experience with phoneticians, especially with Oxford's brilliant and crotchety Henry Sweet. Though Shaw disclaims portraiture and admits to having included no more than touches of Sweet in the play, the reader can sense how Henry Higgins's professional expertise, impatience with fools, and fanatical dedication to the science of speech reflect this Oxford original.

The preface climaxes with a critical bang when Shaw calls the whole play didactic. His citation of its success to "prove" that great art can never be anything but didactic has caused many critics to dismiss him as quixotic. Still, the preface reveals his commitment to a serious aspect of *Pygmalion* and links his life to the play, showing how Higgins reflects his early interest in phonetics, much as Eliza reflects his youthful sensitivity to poverty.

Shaw's original impulse for writing *Pygmalion* had been anything but didactic. As a theater critic, he had frequently critiqued performances of Mrs. Patrick Campbell, whose natural talents, sirenlike stage presence, and mellow voice had made her London's most famous actress next only to Ellen Terry. Shaw expressed more admiration for the lady's magnetism and dexterity than for her acting, but in September 1897, contemplating his *Caesar and Cleopatra*, and noticing that Mrs. Pat was playing Ophelia to Johnston Forbes-Robertson's Hamlet, he wrote Ellen Terry: "I would teach that rapscallionly flower girl of his something. *Caesar and Cleopatra* has been driven clean out of my head by a play I want to write for them in which he shall be a west end gentleman and she an east end dona in an apron and three orange and red ostrich feathers."[1] The flower girl was to lurk at the back of his mind for 15 years. Meanwhile, he composed *Caesar and Cleopatra*, whose youthful, rapscallionly queen was played by Mrs. Pat for a single copyright performance.

Eliza did not take dramatic shape until 1912. Shaw created her for Mrs. Pat. Eliza's howl mocked the actress's temperamental character, her guttersnipe virtue mocked the propriety beneath the actress's seductive veneer, her elegant transformation would indulge the actress's reputation as a siren. But given the fun to be had at Mrs. Pat's expense, as well as Eliza's vulgar beginnings, could the lady be prompted to play the part? To lure his prey, Shaw tried a ruse, reading the play to her. The ruse both worked and backfired: she recognized herself in the role and called him a beast, but then said she was flattered—and he fell "head over ears in love with her."[2]

Their affair lasted for over a year, shaking Shaw's marriage. Mrs. Pat was now "Stella" (her middle name) to him, and he "Joey" (nicknamed after a clown) to her. Shaw wrote her many of the least constrained, most playful, passionate letters of his life, combining tones of an exploitive, machinelike, slightly diabolical, childishly impetuous Higgins with the romancing of a Freddy Eynsford Hill and the critical eye and creative flair of G.B.S.[3] The romance, however, fell upon rocks the next year when Stella jilted him in favor of George Cornwallis-West, an aristocratic version of Freddy. Younger than Shaw, this George was ready to leave his spouse, who happened to be Jennie Churchill, widow of Lord Randolph Churchill and mother of Winston.

Pygmalion did not appear in London for nearly two years. It waited while Stella bickered about leading men, recuperated from a serious traffic accident, and took other theater engagements. Meanwhile, Shaw, having found his plays more enthusiastically received abroad than in England, licensed productions in Vienna and Berlin in the fall of 1913, with the result that German acclaim made London theater managers especially eager for it.

In January 1914 Sir Herbert Beerbohm Tree landed the prize—and the role of Higgins for himself—for his resplendent His Majesty's Theatre. The event was historic: during rehearsals, the stage of His Majesty's became a battlefield for London's last great actor-manager, its most sensational leading actress, and the world's greatest living playwright, egoists all. As an actor, Tree had a fine, intuitive talent and a lively imagination with which he adapted a role to his theatrical instincts, yet as a manager, he flew by the seat of his pants. As an actress, Mrs. Pat was equally intuitive but notoriously demanding and difficult to work with. As a seasoned playwright, critic, and, often, director, Shaw had strong ideas about how his plays should be staged. Fireworks were in order. They rocketed.

After Shaw, Tree became, in effect, the second English critic of *Pygmalion*. His first critique centered on the word *bloody* in act 3: in response to Freddy's offer to walk her across the park, Eliza's gutter-snipe background pops forth: "Walk! Not bloody likely. I am going in a taxi." While Americans have always perceived *bloody* as colloquially English, in England it was a rank vulgarism, as taboo as certain four-letter expletives were (long ago) in America. It had been uttered incidentally in several plays, but never under the spotlight of His

Majesty's. Acutely apprehensive, Tree urged that the word be cut. Shaw refused, stressing its appropriateness and humor. The matter was unsettled until the censor ignored the word. Next, Tree desired a ballroom scene, a spectacle well suited to his immense theater. Shaw vetoed such a scene as superfluous. Finally, Tree pleaded for a romantic ending between Higgins and Eliza, but such froth ran counter to Shaw's intentions. Rehearsals alternately stormed and limped onward.

Prior to the opening night in April, the press learned about the *bloody*. What grist for NEWS—a publicist's dream! Tickets sold rapidly, and the premiere's audience, including over 60 critics, was thoroughly primed. At the age of 42, Mrs. Pat was too old to play Eliza, but years dropped from her as she rose radiantly to the part. The audience cheered her exit in the taxi at the end of act 1. Tree forgot many of his lines but survived by improvising and consulting notes he had distributed around the set. It was an evening of theatrical magic.

The audience kept its composure until Eliza's *bloody* brought a collective gasp, a brief, shocked silence, then exploding laughter, wave upon wave, stopping the show. Shaw left the theater before the final curtain and did not return until the play's one-hundredth performance. With the watchdog gone, Tree took off in all directions, having his romantic way by inflecting lines sentimentally, throwing flowers to Eliza just before the curtain dropped, and, in later performances, having her return prior to the end to ask Higgins about the size of gloves he has ordered. Hearing of Shaw's displeasure, Tree wrote, "My ending makes money: you ought to be grateful." Shaw retorted, "Your ending is damnable: you ought to be shot."[4]

The premiere gave the press a field day. Headlines highlighted the infamous Word: "BERNARD SHAW'S BOLD BAD WORD SPOKEN . . . SENSATION AT HIS MAJESTY'S . . . PROTEST BY DECENCY LEAGUE . . . I SEE NO OBJECTION SAYS PRIME MINISTER . . . SIR HERBERT CENSURED BY THEATRE ASSOCIATION." Dozens of letters to the press condemned the outrage, and only two publications were bold enough to print "the word" in full. Critics disliked its repetition in the play by Clara Eynsford Hill, but her resolve to spread it as "small talk" in fashionable society was mimicked by London society, where it circulated widely, salting second-hand wit.[5]

The *Daily Express* found a Charing Cross flower girl—named Eliza—to attend the premiere and serve as its most colorful critic:

> I never thought I should be so conspic—conspic—well, yer knows wot I mean! . . . It was all rite, though, wen the curten went up. I reely enjoyed meself then, and wen I 'eard the langwidge, it was quite home-like. I never thought as 'ow they allowed sich langwidge on the stige. . . . I thought Mrs Patricia Campbell talked a bit rough. I asked people in the pit if I talked as rough as her, and they said NO, not arf as rough as her. I thought it was funny when she got into the taxi wiv her basket. Of course, flower-girls don't make a habit of getting into taxis, but you know, when you've had a good day, you feels sporty. I didn't like the last bit when Eliza's supposed to fall in love with the Prof. He wanted her to go back to him, yet he didn't say he loved her. It wasn't one thing or another. . . . I wish [Mr Shaw'd] found a better title. Who's ter know *Pygmalion* is anyfing ter do wiv flower-girls?[6]

Many critics of the performance happily took *Pygmalion* as a caper. One remarked, "After the much-wielded threat of its previous success in Germany, one had dreaded something dreadfully portentous. But no! It dances round several important social themes, flashing intelligence on them now and then. But it never attempts to present any 'new gospel' . . . in what is confessedly only a Shavian whimsy."[7]

More originally, H. W. Massingham considered Higgins a defamation of Ovid's Pygmalion. He found Higgins less an artist than a vivisector, a male brute who treats Eliza as a cleverly constructed machine, devitalizing her, merely transforming her slum singsong into the flat dialect of the drawing room. Eliza has not ceased to be a woman, Massingham observed, and when she asks for love and interest and a future, Higgins's response involves little heart or self-understanding. Shaw's play is too cold and unfeeling, and like Eliza, even Doolittle, though almost a masterpiece, talks rather than is. Massingham asked Shaw "what he has made of the soul of Eliza—the coming to herself of this slip of the streets when she realizes the crime which a cold-blooded brute of a scientist had visited upon her."[8]

Most richly suggestive was Desmond MacCarthy, who started with a strong sense of the play's themes beyond Cinderella: "Like all good comedies, it is full of criticism of life; in this case criticism of social barriers and distinctions, of the disinterested yet ferocious egotism of artists, of genteel standards, of the disadvantages of respectability, of the contrast between man's sense of values and woman's." For MacCarthy, the center of interest lies not in the relation between Higgins and Eliza, but in the fact that the molding of a lady in acts 2, 3, and 4 is not the miracle; rather, the miracle occurs in act 5 when Eliza gets a soul and shakes off Higgins to stand on her own feet as an independent human being. Now possessing an inward reality, "the statue has become alive." Unlike Massingham, MacCarthy found that Shaw makes this point, and after finding a vein of Dickens in Doolittle, he perceived Higgins more sensitively than Massingham did, discussing him as a development of Mr. Jack the composer in Shaw's early novel, *Love Among the Artists* (1882), "a study of the creative temperament." Like Jack, Higgins gives his pocket money to a young woman and trains her in elocution, and like Jack, "he has a total disregard of people's feelings, he is outrageously inconsiderate, and yet he is most human. His impatience is the impatience of the artist who only asks Heaven for peace to devote himself to his work."[9]

Strains of these views in response to *Pygmalion*'s London premiere have appeared again and again in the work of later critics, most of whom have seemed unaware that they were anticipated at this early date.

From the beginning, sources for the play have sparked critical interest. Many noticed that its plot parallels an episode in chapter 87 of Smollett's *Peregrine Pickle* (1751), whose heading reads, "Peregrine sets out for the Garrison, and meets with a Nymph of the Road, whom he takes into Keeping and metamorphoses into a fine lady." Others have continued to follow MacCarthy's lead, perceiving sources in Dickens.[10] Further conjectures about sources have run a great gamut from Sir Francis Bacon's *The Advancement of Learning* (1605) to W. S. Gilbert's play *Pygmalion and Galatea* (1871), Ibsen's *A Doll's House*

(1879) and *When We Dead Awaken* (1899), and works by major and minor novelists.[11]

Few have stepped back to observe how this plethora of suggested sources shows not only remarkable faith in the playwright's grasp of contemporary culture, but also, if he was indeed indebted to half of them, his capacity to visit so extensive a heritage on a single comedy. Shaw could not recall having read *Peregrine Pickle* but cared little about whether or not he had: "I may add that if I had read it the result would have been just the same. If I find in a book anything I can make use of, I take it gratefully. My plays are full of pillage of this kind. Shakespeare, Dickens, Conan Doyle, Oscar Wilde, Granville Barker: all is fish that comes to my net. In short, my literary morals are those of Molière and Handel."[12]

The originality of *Pygmalion*'s ending gave Shaw more trouble than its beginnings. Beerbohm Tree's plea for a Higgins-Eliza romance and his sabotage of Shaw's veto by inserting romantic stage business were but opening shots of a long battle. The flower girl who attended the London premiere wanted a frankly affectionate Higgins; London critics tweaked Shaw about his ambiguous conclusion; the manager of the American production adopted Tree's tactics. After all, the play was subtitled "A Romance." Shaw responded: "I call it a romance because it is a story of a poor girl who meets a gentleman at a church door, and is transformed by him, like Cinderella, into a beautiful lady. That is what I call romance. It is also what everybody calls romance; so we are all agreed for once."[13]

But like (or unlike?) Eliza and Higgins, the matter would not go to bed. Attempting to quell sentimentalists, Shaw protested that he could not imagine a less happy ending than marriage between a confirmed bachelor of 40, with a mother complex, and a girl of 18. Nonetheless, German and Dutch films in 1935 and 1937 catered to Cinderellamania by romantically altering his script, and though he kept tighter reins on the 1938 English film, its directors jettisoned his ending as baldly as Tree had.[14] Shaw loathed the first two films but was seen to smile after viewing the English one, and some assumed that he had sheathed his antiromantic hatchet. Hardly. Never one to cry over spilt milk, he was being a good sport. In 1948 a publicist for the Minneapolis Civic Theater wrote him: "Controversy rages over ending. Shall we . . . make villagers happy or shall we leave them in Shavian suspension?" He shot back that he absolutely forbade "any suggestion that the middleaged bully and the girl of eighteen are lovers."[15]

Still, the Civic Theater ignored his words, and enthusiasm for *Pygmalion* à la Cinderella persisted. In 1949 a Stanford professor dignified the popular drift: "'Pygmalion' is shameless art for art's sake, a fairy tale told with relentless logic and realism." Two years later an essay in the English profession's leading journal explained that the play is a classic, old-fashioned comedy. In 1956 a biographer declared that "the facts of the play cry out against the author," since the ends of acts 4 and 5 "assure all sensible people that she married Henry Higgins and bore him many vigorous and intelligent children." That same year Alan Jay Lerner justified *My Fair Lady*: "The end of the play, I hope, satisfies the desire of seeing them together. . . . Music can do that because music can put you in a mood to accept it as inevitable." And in 1973 Maurice Valency, robed in his years as a critic, roundly condemned the play's perversity: "*Pygmalion* fizzles out in a *Doll's House* type of discussion which is never resolved. . . . It is difficult to imagine anything artistically more inept than a rationalistic conclusion of the Cinderella story. . . . A love scene at the end of the play was really obligatory."[16]

Such bombardments could lead one to suspect that Shaw had been beaten from the field. But not so. Since World War II, counterattacks by critics defending his cause have exposed Valency and others as critical dinosaurs to whom stage conventions were more real than life. In 1947 the spirit of Massingham and MacCarthy reemerged in Eric Bentley, whose book on Shaw has become a classic: "The fifth act of *Pygmalion* is far from superfluous. It is the climax. The arousing of Eliza's resentment in the fourth Act was the birth of a soul. But to be born is not enough. One must also grow up. . . . Eliza has now become not only a person but an independent person."[17]

To Bentley and a rising tide of critics, the issues of Eliza's "soul" and maturation move the play into a spiritual dimension whose central action lies less in heartthrobs, a ball-scene climax, and a valentine ending than in the importance of Eliza's growth as she evolves from a flower girl to the image of a lady in acts 1 through 3, then to womanhood in acts 4 and 5. Contrary to Valency's complaint, many have seen Eliza's growth as indeed similar to the illumination and final independence of Nora Helmer in *A Doll's House*.[18]

Besides these links to the spiritual qualities that make *A Doll's House* a pioneering feminist play, several modern critics have seen *Pygmalion* as feminist quite apart from any connection it may have to Ibsen.[19] Others take another tack by highlighting the spiritual aspects of Higgins's role.[20] A middle ground between the extremes marked by those who stress Eliza's self-creation and those who stress Higgins as her creator is taken by some who, like J. L. Wisenthal, appreciate both her life force and Higgins's role in helping her realize it,[21] a view that stirs up the famous question at the end of the play: Will Eliza marry the professor? Most critics now agree with Shaw: not bloody likely. Several, however, qualify this view by taking a sensible textual tack, noting that Shaw's original ending, which left the romantic issue hanging, was discreetly tantalizing and artistic but was unfortunately buried by the fervor of Eliza-Higgins romantics on the one hand and by Shaw's attempts to beat them down on the other.[22]

Paradoxically, current antiromantic interpretations of Pygmalion have engaged in overkill by failing to observe that myths are indeed important to the play.[23] None has closely addressed the fact that Shaw himself cited its Cinderella motif, and not until the past 15 years have several plumbed the play's title beyond Massingham's belief that Higgins is a defamation of Ovid's legend and Bentley's comment that, unlike the original Pygmalion, who turns a statue into a human being, Higgins tries to turn a human being into a statue.[24] Few have followed up on Louis Crompton's comment that Higgins possesses a "Promethean passion" or probed Shaw's fertile use of other myths in the play.

The neglect of links between *Pygmalion* and its mythical antecedents is but one of many gaps in the play's critical history. The gap between critics who stress Eliza's self-creation and those who stress Higgins as her creator has been only partially filled, and an immense gap between Cinderella romantics and Shavian naturalists remains. Then, too, Shaw's preface declaration that the play is about phonetics has been largely bypassed, though a few have addressed his interest in phonetics, language, and alphabet reform.[25] More thought about Shaw's preface might suggest how the social importance of phonetics provides links across many of these critical voids. Reviewing the film in 1939, MacCarthy once again explained this better than most: "The theme of Pygmalion is as fresh as it was; namely, that class-distinctions are uncivilised; that the worst manners spring from class-consciousness, and class-consciousness from differences in pronunciation and accent."[26]

Other gaps might have been crossed by psychological analyses of *Pygmalion*'s characters, but unfortunately, such delving has focused more on Shaw than on the play. The gist of several recent analyses is that Eliza personifies Shaw's mother and Higgins personifies Vandeleur Lee, her voice teacher. To fend off thoughts about his possible illegitimacy as Lee's son, the argument goes, Shaw ruled out sex between his heroine and hero. Further prying uncaps an incest fantasy: Higgins's Oedipus complex reflects Shaw's. Like the mythical Pygmalion who created Galatea then married her, Higgins "fathers" his creation, making her into a lady like his (and Shaw's) mother. Eliza also represents Mrs. Patrick Campbell, calling up Shaw's thwarted love of the actress. Thus, in a cacophonous compendium of concupiscence, Higgins may be both Shaw and Shaw's natural father, while Eliza offers Shaw the titillating possibility of union with daughter, mother, and Stella Campbell all in one.[27]

Shaw responded to such Freudology with little more than a "So what?" Prior to writing *Pygmalion*, he candidly admitted to an Oedipus complex and disparaged the trauma about it in Sophocles' *Oedipus Rex*. Later he advised a "sex-obsessed Biographer" that his sex history would show only that he was human. Over 99 percent of him, he observed, was commonplace; the difficulty was to locate and describe the distinguishing half percent.[28]

In short, the history of diverse, often contentious approaches to *Pygmalion* signals both its delights and its depths. While 99 percent of the public may simply relish its romantic echoes and comedy, serious critics mine it variously for the half percent that makes Shaw extraordinary. Disparate as the public and critical viewpoints may be, each is telling. Widespread appetites for myth and laughter may not be sharply discriminating, but in appealing to them the play has delighted the world—no small matter. And hardly less important are the critical perceptions of Eliza's spiritual growth and of Higgins's remarkable character, as well as the issues of social class, science, art, economics, psychology, phonetics, and education raised by the play. A critical problem between these views occurs when one discards or ignores others without a fair hearing, as romantics have often done by throwing out Shaw, and as Shavian critics have tried to do by throwing out romance.

Is there a middle ground? Can there be a middle ground? Besides crisscrossing the issues mentioned above, the following will aim at a surprising gap in the argument of many who focus on Eliza's spiritual growth. In 1914 H. W. Massingham spoke of Eliza "coming to herself," and Desmond MacCarthy said that "in Act V something happened, she had got a soul." Since then, few have been more specific about just how Eliza gets a soul. The process, a fascinating one, can tie together many popular and critical aspects of the play. Let's take a look.

A READING

HIS MAJESTY'S THEATRE
HERBERT TREE
PYGMALION

Poster for the first English production, 1914.

4

Act 1: The Awakening

Not long before *Pygmalion*'s first London performance, the English caricaturist Max Beerbohm cartooned Shaw and himself: Beerbohm stands at one side, his eyebrows and fingers raised apprehensively as he views Shaw—who is standing on his head. The caption reads: "Mild surprise of one who, revisiting England after long absence, finds that the dear fellow has not moved."

Touché! Since Shaw was notorious for turning things topsy-turvy, the world might well have fancied him upside down. In politics, social affairs, religion, and many other matters, his upside-downness could be disconcerting, diverting, maddening, or comic, a bit like that of Father William in Lewis Carroll's *Alice's Adventures in Wonderland* (1865), who apparently stands on his head out of crotchety perversity. Yet unlike Father William, Shaw's upside-downness was a way of finding fresh—and thus, perhaps, clearer—perspectives on the world. Upside-downness could be literally revolutionary. Albert Einstein, for example, had recently revolutionized modern physics with the theory of relativity, a topsy-turvy notion that the essence of what we observe relates not just to things themselves but also to their relation to everything else, including their relation to the observer, space and time being not absolutes but relative to all sorts of movement and frames of reference.

Shaw personified relativity: he might have seemed topsy-turvy to ordinary folk, but then geniuses may be right side up while less thoughtful people who think themselves right side up may in fact be upside down. Ever since humans knew that the earth was flat because their eyes told them so, science, philosophy, and art have shown the value of uncommon sense, and Shaw declared himself a case in point.

For instance, he found that dramas often end with an episode that could make the beginning of a more interesting play. Thus, *Pygmalion* starts with an ending, and the apparent conclusiveness of its first act is but a prelude to its second. The end at the play's beginning is the conclusion of a theater performance, not just after the fantasy onstage has vanished behind a final curtain, but after the applause, the bows, and the raising of the auditorium's lights, when the audience has crowded through exits, only to find a heavy rainstorm outside. Suddenly, soggy realities drown theatrical illusions. Keeping dry becomes everyone's priority, and dryness demands handy transportation, a special problem for audiences in cities like London where taxis, otherwise plentiful, seem to scurry about attending to other people's needs, disappearing when theater mobs desire them most. This challenge tests one's nimbleness, aggressiveness, and savoir faire: hailing a cab amid a cab-hungry throng is a business of everybody for himself—survival of the fittest.

Besides launching *Pygmalion* with a post-theater scene that his audience can keenly appreciate, and thereby connecting the audience to its counterpart inside the play and to the outside world, Shaw uses the scene's chaos to characterize three persons. Some hearty males may relish the competition of hailing taxis, but there are always the poor souls who seem to be the last in any crowd to secure a taxi or anything else. For these, the turmoil can be daunting, humiliating. While reluctance to outjostle others should be a sign of gentility, in males it suggests a wimp in evening clothes—an especially mortifying impression if the wimp has ladies in tow. The ladies themselves may be better at chasing taxis, but true ladies with escorts do not do such things. They can only despair, pitying or scorning the ineffectual male, perhaps even longing (heaven forbid) for machismo.

Act 1: Eliza's Awakening

Such is the case with the threesome Shaw presents: a middle-aged lady, her daughter, and her taxi-chasing son. For all we know, they may never appear again. They may exist just to set a mood. After all, the guards at the start of *Hamlet* only introduce a ghost, and Hollywood throws up extras like confetti. Shaw, however, makes the most of each minute. The dilemma of these three conveys a mood, introduces a theme, and provides a background for a crucial role they will play later on. Here, they are tested by a scarcity of taxis; later they will be central to a test of the play's heroine. Since the genteel setting at that time will call for their best behavior, now they are exposed as a family group with their guards down. This exposure is also important because they represent a certain segment of society and because the son who now pursues taxis will soon pursue the play's heroine.

Amid the helter-skelter, the lady and her daughter peer out gloomily from under the portico of St. Paul's Church in Covent Garden. Their dialogue resembles a duet, a frequent characteristic in Shaw's plays, harking from his years as a music critic: the daughter is a soprano, impatient, abrasive; the mother, an alto, is distressed but apologetic, sympathetic:

THE DAUGHTER. . . . What can Freddy be doing all this time? He's been gone twenty minutes.

THE MOTHER. . . . Not so long. But he ought to have got us a cab by this. . . .

THE DAUGHTER. If Freddy had a bit of gumption, he would have got one at the theatre door.

THE MOTHER. What could he have done, poor boy?

THE DAUGHTER. Other people get cabs. Why couldnt he?

Umbrella dripping, feet soaked, the young gentleman rushes in, full of excuses, creating a trio:

THE DAUGHTER. Well, havnt you got a cab?

FREDDY. Theres not one to be had for love or money. . . . Ive been to Charing Cross one way and nearly to Ludgate Circus the other; and they were all engaged.

THE MOTHER. Did you try Trafalgar Square?

FREDDY. There wasnt one at Trafalgar Square.

THE DAUGHTER. Did you try? . . .

The women join in browbeating him:

THE MOTHER. You really are very helpless, Freddy. Go again; and dont come back until you have found a cab.

FREDDY. I shall simply get soaked for nothing.

THE DAUGHTER. And what about us? . . . You selfish pig—

FREDDY. Oh, very well: I'll go, I'll go.

This trio climaxes when Freddy dashes off, only to collide with a flower girl, knocking her basket from her hands, and "*a blinding flash of lightning, followed instantly by a rattling peal of thunder, orchestrates the incident*" (13–15).

The simultaneous lightning, thunder, and collision may briefly thrill romantics in the audience, but the spectacular contrast of these events with the play's realistic opening should spark amusement. As in romantic opera or melodrama, Zeus pops forth, a cosmic flasher. With the action rolling onward, the audience can scarcely ask why, yet it has been jolted by an omen, a flash of fun that starts a fanciful obbligato. From this point on, fancy complements the play's realism, sometimes rising through it, often playing against or over it. Also starting here are themes that reappear in various keys throughout the play. The importance of a taxi is one; Freddy's claim that no cab is to be had "for love or money" heralds others; and his sister calling him a "selfish pig" anticipates the eventual role of these three as guinea pigs.

The sensational collision of Freddy and the flower girl highlights two who are separated by an immense social gulf, the young gentleman sheltered by his class as well as by his umbrella, the girl sheltered by neither. Her slangy exclamation, "Nah then, Freddy: look wh' y' gowin, deah," contrasts sharply with what she is to become, while his scarcely pausing to say a simple "Sorry" shows ever so much less consideration than he would give a lady and contrasts with his lovestruck pursuit of her when she appears as a lady later on.

Accentuating the contrast between them is his clothing and hers. To warn directors who might be inclined to glamorize the girl beneath mere tokens of shabby attire (a flattery that later appeared in the play's film version), Shaw specifies that she is *"not at all a romantic figure."* Cataloging her squalor, from her dusty, sooty, black straw sailor hat to her seldom-brushed, mouse-colored hair, shoddy black coat, brown skirt, coarse apron, and badly worn boots, he notes that her features may be no worse than the ladies' but she is very dirty by comparison, and he concludes with a minute but graphic detail that drives home her poverty: *"She needs the services of a dentist"* (15–16).

Separating the gentlefolk and the flower girl even more profoundly is their speech. For the better part of his life, Shaw campaigned for a phonetic alphabet. Lacking one, he could only suggest the girl's cockney in her first short speeches. To the mother's question, "How do you know that my son's name is Freddy, pray?" she replies, "Ow, eez ya-ooa san is e? Wal fewd dan y' da-ooty bawmz a mather should, eed now bettern to spawl a pore gel's flahrzn than ran awy athaht pyin. Will ye-oo py me f'them?" Her words reveal how stereotypes and contrasts can take bizarre turns. What she says, as opposed to how she speaks, links her with the mother. Translating the words, we have, "Oh, he's your son is he? Well, if you'd done your duty by him as a mother should, he'd know better than to spoil a poor girl's flowers and then run away without paying. Will you pay me for them?"

For all her dirtiness and poverty, the girl's sentiments and request reflect a keen sense of courtesy, propriety, and responsibility.

These civilized characteristics place her on a higher level of humanity than the daughter, who chooses snobbery over civility: "Do nothing of the sort, mother. The idea!" (17).

The daughter's reluctance to give her mother sixpence for the girl and her niggardly demand for a few pennies' change are explained, with interest, later in the play; here, the mother's readiness to forgo the change masks a hidden agenda: "Now tell me how you know that young gentleman's name." The girl's explanation that she called him "Freddy" or "Charlie" much as the mother might in being pleasant to a stranger reveals both her innocent, kindly intentions and her lower-class unawareness that a lady would never use familiar nicknames in addressing a stranger. The daughter's following exclamation—"Sixpence thrown away! Really, mamma, you might have spared Freddy that"—clarifies the mother's generosity. Apparently the lady has some reason to fear a shady relationship between her son and flower girls, another concern that takes an ironic turn before the end of the play.

This episode's crisscrossing class distinctions and many links to forthcoming events introduce the compact, allusive quality of *Pygmalion*'s dramatic art. Shaw wastes no time. Every character, action, and virtually every word, including many that seem incidental at a given moment, builds toward effects, themes, and characterizations in the whole play. Although each detail's relation to the rest is not immediately apparent, the interweaving of details becomes part of the audience's total experience as the play unfolds, adding depth and dramatic power to the development of characters and themes.

The play's main action begins with the arrival of an *"elderly gentleman of the amiable military type"* who, like the family, wears evening dress and seeks shelter. Much as she had done with Freddy, the girl addresses him by habit in a familiar street-vendor fashion. Her calling him "Captain," however, places him a notch above those she would call "Freddy," and once again money—now becoming a theme—draws lines of class. Whereas the daughter and mother had nothing less than sixpence, the gentleman believes that he has nothing less than a sovereign. Sizing him up as a better customer than they, the girl makes no distinctions between enterprise, survival, and honesty in offering him a flower (according to the daughter, "only a penny a bunch") for twopence. He hardly wants to bother—"I'm sorry. I havnt any change"—but considerately tries his pockets, coming up with three halfpence. As he (unlike the daughter) clearly expects nothing in return, a bystander warns the girl of someone who has been standing at the periphery of the action, writing in a notebook. Apparently a gentleman's casual kindness can get a poor girl in trouble: "You be careful: give him a flower for it. Theres a bloke here behind taking down every blessed word youre saying" (17–19).

With this, Shaw catapults the action into a Scene:

THE FLOWER GIRL [*springing up terrified*] I aint done nothing wrong by speaking to the gentleman. Ive a right to sell flowers if I keep off the kerb. [*Hysterically*] I'm a respectable girl: so help me, I never spoke to him except to ask him to buy a flower off me.

> *General hubbub, mostly sympathetic to the flower girl, but deprecating her excessive sensibility. Cries of* Dont start hollerin. Who's hurting you? Nobody's going to touch you. Whats the good of fussing? Steady on. Easy easy, etc., *come from the elderly staid spectators, who pat her comfortingly. Less patient ones bid her shut her head, or ask her roughly what is wrong with her. . . .*

THE FLOWER GIRL [*breaking through them to the gentleman, crying wildly*] Oh, sir, dont let him charge me. You dunno what it means to me. Theyll take away my character and drive me on the streets for speaking to gentlemen. They— (19–20)

The varied responses to the girl's hysteria give texture and realism to the hubbub. This is a crowd of individuals, not just a theatrical mob. And most telling are personal and social revelations in the girl's terror. She believes she is confronting the Law: "I aint done nothing wrong. . . . Oh, sir, dont let him charge me." For one of her profession and social station, the law is clearly less a protector than a power that threatens her existence, a monster whose rules must be followed to the letter. It determines right and wrong, and she clings to the niggling rights it grants: "Ive a right to sell flowers if I keep off the kerb." By keeping her off the curb, the law, and the gentlefolk it supports, literally consign her to the gutter, yet she considers herself above the gutter—that is, above prostitution, a profession far more lucrative for poor girls than selling violets: "I'm a respectable girl. . . . I never spoke to him except to ask him to buy a flower off me." Gentlefolk don't know what arrest would mean to her: "Theyll take away my character" (the police will accuse her of prostitution) "and drive me on the streets" (ironically, they will deprive her of her right to sell flowers so that she may indeed be forced into prostitution), merely "for speaking to gentlemen." And ironically again, "on the streets" connotes prostitution, while her "character" and being "respectable" put her in the gutter.

While all of the girl's clothing befits the gutter (prostitution could give her better attire), footwear alone prompts the bystander to allay her fears: "It's aw rawt: e's a genleman: look at his ba-oots." So small a detail, so great a distinction. The note taker, in turn, commands the "silly girl" to "shut up" and shows her his strange script, which he reads aloud as her dialect: "Cheer ap, Keptin; n' baw ya flahr orf a pore gel" (20–22).

As this echoes the misunderstanding over her use of "Freddy" with the young gentleman, she is once again panicked: "It's because I called him Captain." The elderly gentleman and the crowd take her side but are nonplussed when the note taker identifies her origins as Lisson Grove, far across London. And class raises its head again when she describes Lisson Grove as not fit for a pig to live in, though costly for her scant means. The elderly gentleman comforts her kindly, "You have a right to live where you please," only to be countered by a sarcastic bystander: "Park Lane, for instance. I'd like to go into the Housing Question with you, I would" (22–23).

Incidentally, but pointedly, another theme! The "Housing Question," illustrated by the chasm between the luxurious town houses of Park Lane and the squalid tenements of Lisson Grove, came readily to the lips of social reformers, much as slums concern reformers today. The grim question—grist for studies, reports, and political contention—would hardly seem suited to comedy. Yet Shaw makes it part of the social scene along with concerns about taxis, manners, a mother's duty, money, dress, the law, prostitution, character, idiom, and dialect, a cluster of subjects even more diverse than the crowd that huddles around the flower girl. As in a kaleidoscope, each subject jostles others, and as all are turned by the dramatic action, their shifting patterns provide colorfully graphic views of class disparities.

In the next eight minutes, the action and allusions become even more complex as Shaw variously counterpoints the note taker, the flower girl, the elderly gentleman, the mother, the daughter, and the bystanders. Now, however, he views social distinctions through a very specific lens. While the flower girl says to herself, "I'm a good girl, I am," a plaintive echo of her earlier declaration that "I take my Bible oath I never said a word" (she's virtuous and honorable), the sarcastic bystander challenges the note taker: "Do you know where *I* come from?" The prompt response, "Hoxton," increases *"popular interest in the note taker's performance"* (24).

"Performance" describes the situation aptly, yet it also amounts to an intellectual sales pitch and a show within a show, played not only for the crowd onstage but also for *Pygmalion*'s audience. Hooked from the sidelines (and hooking the audience), the note taker moves to center stage, dramatically highlighting what might otherwise seem a tedious academic subject—phonetics—which Shaw makes fascinating both through gripping illustrations and its relationship to matters of class. After the note taker identifies the modest origins of bystanders as well as the flower girl according to their speech, they dare him to do the same with the elderly gentleman: "You take us for dirt under your feet, dont you? Catch you taking liberties with a gentleman!"—"Yes: tell him where he come from if you want to go fortune-telling." Undaunted, he replies, "Cheltenham, Harrow, Cambridge, and India." This moves far beyond neighborhoods to elite schooling and colonial experience. Its dazzling scope, and the fact that its uncanniness links the gentlemen to them, spur the crowd to laughter and exclamations of wonder—a response *Pygmalion*'s audience can share, so that wonder mirrors wonder.

Building upon the reaction, Shaw has the gentleman ask, "Do you do this for your living at a music hall?" The note taker's performance, after all, reminds one of awesome memory wizards, jugglers, acrobats, and tricksters. The rain stops, the crowd starts to disperse, but not the play's audience, now engaged by dramatic legerdemain: both on stage and off, this entertainment conveys an academic lesson. Spontaneous delight prompts curiosity, the best prod of learning.

A measure of dramatic craftsmanship more noticed in its breach than in its smooth execution is the naturalness with which a playwright moves characters on and off stage to provide successive groupings. Through the playwright's godly powers, Shaw uses a rainstorm to cluster otherwise diverse persons under the church portico, and the storm's end to move most of them away. Yet to abridge an artificial exodus and characterize key players further, he provides natural concluding actions, first with the mother and daughter, then with the bystander and the sarcastic bystander, juxtaposing these with the note taker and the elderly gentleman and counterpointing them all with self-centered bleats from the flower girl.

More than before, the daughter reveals how a lady may undercut her gentility by asserting it too strongly. Out of patience, she pushes her way rudely to the front, "*displacing the gentleman, who politely retires to the other side of the pillar*": "What on earth is Freddy doing? I shall get pneumownia if I stay in this draught any longer." Her pronunciation of *monia* stirs the professionalism of the note taker, who jots it down as "Earlscourt," much as he identifies her mother's dialect as "Epsom." The daughter cuts him off—"Will you please keep your impertinent remarks to yourself"— but her mother deflects her crassness by advancing with gentle interest and an open mind: "How very curious! I was brought up in Largelady Park, near Epsom." The note taker returns courtesy for the daughter's curtness, begging her pardon, yet slips as he roars at "Largelady Park": "Ha! ha! what a devil of a name! Excuse me" (25).

Since Earlscourt was respectable but much less fashionable than other quarters of London or Epsom, a resort to the south, there is a hint that the mother and daughter have declined on the social ladder, a circumstance nettling the daughter. At the same time, Shaw exploits the English penchant for colorful place names by associating the mother with a landed estate of large (both esteemed *and* ample?) ladies. The note taker's hilarity highlights the name play, his delight in words, and his indecorous impulsiveness. To compensate for his intemperance, he makes equally spontaneous amends: in contrast to the ineffectual Freddy, he hails a cab for the two with the piercing blast of a whistle. Within moments, this action elicits further distinctions. The sarcastic bystander tries to reduce his status—"There! I knowed he was a plain-clothes copper"—only to be countered by the bystander: "That aint a police whistle: thats a sporting whistle." When the note taker points out that the rain has stopped, the discourtesy of the bystanders resembles the daughter's, though their dialects place them below her socially. One exclaims about time lost "listening to your silliness," the other sneers, "I can tell where you come from. You come from Anwell [a mental institution]. Go back there." The insult backfires when the note taker helpfully suggests "*H*anwell." Attempting one-upmanship, the undercut man witlessly one-downs himself linguistically as he strolls off, "*affecting great distinction of speech*": "Thenk you, teacher. Haw haw! So long." What the bystanders have not learned about themselves, the audience has.

In a casual detail that subtly anticipates the play's comic highlight (in act 3), the mother gathers her skirts and hurries off, commenting, "It's quite fine now, Clara. We can walk to a motor bus," to which the daughter responds, "But the cab— Oh, how tiresome!" Compelled to walk, the young lady follows angrily.

Equally subtle is a striking example of dramatic doubleness when the flower girl, arranging her basket and caught in self-pity, murmurs, "Poor girl! Hard enough for her to live without being worried and chivied." Her speech cuts two ways: it reflects her own plight yet also serves as a coda to the vignette of the mother and daughter. The mother does not find walking to a motor bus demeaning. Like the flower girl, the daughter, more defensive about her status, is worried and "chivied" (bothered by little repeated attacks on her dignity). Except for a small expense, why not take a cab? One may remember the ladies' earlier contention over sixpence and change. Was that mere cheapness, or did it signal something else? Can a lady be a lady if she niggles over change, or chooses walking and motor buses rather than taxis? The action sweeps past such questions now, but Shaw plants them, like small land mines, for future explosions.

With the crowd and the ladies offstage, the gentleman asks, like a spectator at a magic show (and on behalf of *Pygmalion*'s audience), "How do you do it, if I may ask?" The note taker's answer is almost as impressive as his magic: "Simply phonetics. The science of speech. Thats my profession: also my hobby. Happy is the man who can make a living by his hobby! You can spot an Irishman or a Yorkshireman by his brogue. *I* can place any man within six miles. I can place him within two miles in London. Sometimes within two streets" (26).

This may seem uncanny. It is certainly less possible in America than in England, where the pronunciation of words still reflects ancient shires or populations native to urban locales. Modern migrations have lessened phonetic distinctions since the time of the play, yet a skilled phonetician can indeed muster vestiges of the note taker's talent even in the United States, where a speaker's origins may be identified by speech sounds according to areas of the country and even according to some cities and neighborhoods. Novices, for example, can tell a native of the South, the Northeast, and the Midwest, natives of Boston or New York City, or areas in New York City, and many middle-aged Americans can distinguish between the phonetics of Presidents Truman, Kennedy, Johnson, Carter, and Clinton.

Shaw's note taker is a linguist and dialectician as well as a phonetician. Earlier, when the bystander explained that the girl thought him "a copper's nark," he took quick interest in the unusual word: "Whats a copper's nark?" The bystander fumbled, "It's a—well, it's a copper's nark, as you might say. What else would you call it? A sort of informer" (21). Such a word could help identify the speaker's origin. Similarly, in the United States some northeasterners may refer to a crisp doughnut as a cruller, a term relatively unknown in the West. What natives south of the Mason-Dixon Line call a bucket, many north of the line call a pail. Word usage in the West is more heterogeneous, but a westerner who recognizes that "chesterfield" signifies a davenport or couch is likely either to have Canadian ancestors or to come from Eureka, California, where a furniture dealer from Canada once promoted couches as "chesterfields." Thus, while speech sounds are the note taker's specialty, his bag has tricks besides phonetics.

When the gentleman asks, "But is there a living in that?" phonetics takes on practical teeth: "Oh yes. Quite a fat one. This is an age of upstarts. Men begin in Kentish Town with £80 a year, and end in Park Lane with a hundred thousand. They want to drop Kentish Town; but they give themselves away every time they open their mouths." The bite of this may be less sharp today, but what upstart or yuppie can be unaware of dialect conformity in many boardrooms, clubs, societies, or on television and radio, including attitudes that dialects may provoke?

Shaw makes the point swiftly, then catapults it after the flower girl complains, "Let him mind his own business and leave a poor girl—":

THE NOTE TAKER [*explosively*] Woman: cease this detestable boohooing instantly; or else seek the shelter of some other place of worship.

THE FLOWER GIRL [*with feeble defiance*] Ive a right to be here if I like, same as you.

THE NOTE TAKER. A woman who utters such depressing and disgusting sounds has no right to be anywhere—no right to live. Remember that you are a human being with a soul and the divine gift of articulate speech: that your native language is the language of Shakespear and Milton and The Bible; and dont sit there crooning like a bilious pigeon. (27)

Although this outburst at least promotes her to a "woman," it takes a quantum leap beyond the note taker's short patience at the "silly girl" some minutes before. "No right to *live*"? Whence such a brutal blast? Impulsively, he is venting his irritation at being nagged by the girl's hysteria, her repeated assertions of her character and rights, her complaints and pouting and muttering. More deeply, his perceptions of the situation, of realities, of life itself, are worlds apart from hers. To him, her desperate fear of ruin and declarations of propriety and dignity are simply nonsense, and to his sensitive professional ear her very sounds are mortally offensive.

Still, he has not noticed that the girl's responses reveal that she too has a sharp ear: after he had identified the origins of the gentleman, she declared that the note taker was "no gentleman . . . to interfere with a poor girl" (25); after he had spoken respectfully to the ladies and hailed a cab for them, she whimpered, "My character is the same to me as any lady's" (26). And the subject of where she might live has come up before. To her boo-hoo-oo-ing he had responded, "Live where you like; but stop that noise," whereas the gentleman consoled her, "You have a right to live where you please" (23). Now she asserts her right to be (to live) right here, just as he is caught up in explaining his profession. He might respond with an impetuous "Aggghh!" but he respects articulation too much. Rights? Whose *rights*? Her disgusting, depressing sounds violate his sense of language, of meaningful existence, of the articulation that distinguishes a human soul.

Suddenly, we may perceive that the church portico serves not just for local color or as a convenient shelter but also as an exalted sounding board. A spiritual element glimmered first when the flower girl took her "Bible oath" that she never said an illicit word to the gentleman. Now it comes to the fore when the note taker calls attention to the place of worship, then uses the power and glory of language to admonish her. His terms take flight: "Remember that you are a *human being* with a *soul* and the *divine gift* of articulate speech." The point, illustrated with the language of Shakespeare, Milton, and "The" (King James) Bible, amounts to little less than a profession of his faith and a small sermon. Pitted not only against the note taker's eloquence but also against Shakespeare, Milton, and The Bible, the girl, "*quite overwhelmed, looking up at him in mingled wonder and deprecation without daring to raise her head*," half-whines, half-howls, less like a gutter-dwelling pigeon than a beast: "Ah-ah-ah-ow-ow-ow-oo!"

The contrast between the note taker's gift of articulate speech and her noise climaxes his point dramatically. Shifting from aversion to professional fascination, he whips out his book, writes, then reads her vowels exactly. Her reaction—laughter and "Garn!" in spite of herself—breaks her intimidation. In a flash, she grows beyond hysteria and self-pity. Her awe separated them; now her laughter, a self-expression above words, momentarily joins them. As she assimilates speech from those about her, so does he. He has mimicked something specifically, oddly her own, reproducing her inflections like a phonograph. His mimicry is outrageous, funny, and, given her acquisitive, survivalist mind, educational.

Further education follows close upon her laugh, though at first it is addressed to the gentleman, not her:

THE NOTE TAKER. You see this creature with her kerbstone English: the English that will keep her in the gutter to the end of her days. Well, sir, in three months I could pass that girl off as a duchess at an ambassador's garden party. I could even get her a place as a lady's maid or shop assistant, which requires better English.

THE FLOWER GIRL. What's that you say?

THE NOTE TAKER. Yes, you squashed cabbage leaf, you disgrace to the noble architecture of these columns, you incarnate insult to the English language. I could pass you off as the Queen of Sheba. (27–28)

Her laughter having purged her wounded pride, the girl's simple "What's that you say?" signals her awakening to a hitherto unheard-of possibility. Keenly aware of her place down off the curb, in the gutter, she is streetwise and squashed enough to have no hopes of nobility, but canny enough to hear that within three months good English could get her a place as a lady's maid or a shop assistant. The note taker's context has descended from the heavens and Shakespeare to a level she can appreciate. Be it only a crack, a door has opened and light shines through.

Meanwhile the gentlemen utterly forget her when they discover that they know each other by reputation, each having planned to meet the other as a fellow professional: Colonel Pickering from India, the author of *Spoken Sanscrit*, and Henry Higgins, author of *Higgins's Universal Alphabet*. As they go off for supper, the flower girl, ever resourceful and having just heard that Pickering is staying at the Carlton (a luxury hotel), tries to sell him a flower for the sake of her own humbler bed: "I'm short for my lodging." Shocked, Higgins observes, "Liar. You said you could change half-a-crown." So much for commercial enterprise and compassion. The act has come full circle back to money and lodging, wealth versus poverty, honor versus dishonor. Frustrated, she flings the basket at Higgins's feet: "Take the whole blooming basket for sixpence" (the same amount she had from the mother).

Much as lightning and thunder marked her collision with Freddy, now the church clock strikes. *"Hearing in it the voice of God, rebuking him for his Pharisaic want of charity,"* Higgins remarks, "A reminder. [*He raises his hat solemnly; then throws a handful of money into the basket and follows Pickering*]."

Thus, fanciful signs from heaven near the start of the act and near its end enclose phonetics, issues of class, and a plethora of other worldly concerns. Yet there has been a dramatic shift in divinity and charity. Formerly, the Grecian columns of the portico echoed classical antiquity as the lightning and thunder echoed Zeus, with the girl hawking flowers for pennies eked from penny-pinchers. Now the church has been defined by Higgins, who fancies God in the bells of its clock, and his treasure tumbles forth, so little to him, so much to her. Social contrasts remain: change that he throws away amounts to a fortune for the girl, whose howls reflect the relative value of the coins. And enclosing the heavenly wonders is Freddy's pursuit of taxis. Bringing one at last, his ignominy climaxes: the ladies have gone "and left me with a cab on my hands! Damnation!"

Even in success Freddy is a loser. Ladies condemned him before; now it's up to a flower girl to save him, *"with grandeur,"* as she declares, "Never mind, young man. *I*'m going home in a taxi." The tables have turned: now he is a "young man," and she will ride, he will walk. This lady manqué is almost tripped up when the cabbie holds the door shut against her until she shows him her heaven-sent wealth: "A taxi fare aint no object to me, Charlie." There is no casual "Sorry" from Freddy now. Reflecting Higgins's raising of his hat to God, the dazed young man raises his hat to her, saying "Goodbye" much as he might to a lady, whereupon she climaxes her ruse by directing the cabbie: "Bucknam Pellis [Buckingham Palace]" (28–29).

*　　　　*　　　　*

Act 1: Eliza's Awakening

The flower girl's actual destination—"Angel Court, Drury Lane, next Meiklejohn's oil shop"—reveals another play on place names when she arrives at a dreary lane of Drury Lane, hardly a court of angels. The humble locale puts this "lady" in her place, as does her complaint about the shilling taxi fare (echoing the daughter's earlier objection to sixpence for flowers). The driver asks, "Ever been in a taxi before?" To her extravagant attempt at dignity—"Hundreds and thousands of times, young man"—he laughs, "Good for you, Judy. Keep the shilling, darling, with best love from all at home. Good luck!" and drives off (30). Charged with innuendo, his "Judy" matches her lower-class slip in calling him "Charlie." His "keep the shilling, darling" exudes condescending charity; his "best love from all at home" mocks her breezily with an upper-class touch of those who can afford foreign travels; and his "Good luck" admires her audacity, wishing her well against immense odds.

The audience may join in his perception and sympathize with the dwindling ladyhood in her humiliated reaction—"Impidence!" The sympathy should increase as Shaw details the squalor of her small room (made less wretched by directors of the film version) and her counting of her new riches before she climbs into bed, under her shawl and skirt, so that she can dream and plan more cheaply and warmly.

The novelistic quality of this final scene appears more subtly earlier when "the note taker" and "the gentleman" become "Higgins" and "Pickering" only after their dialogue identifies them by name. Such a tactic is common in Shaw's plays: if a character's name does not appear in an opening stage direction, Shaw usually provides a generic identification until the character is named in the course of the action. The practice originated partly from his early experience as a novelist, but more from the fact that most of his early plays were published before they were performed. To encourage a play-reading public, he favored novelistic touches over the theatrical shorthand of most playscripts. Yet the tactic also has a theatrical purpose, offering actors and directors clues about the nature of characters and the performance of a scene, and giving characters and action dramatic life for readers by unfolding them in print much as audiences would experience them in a performance. Thus, the identification of Higgins and Pickering comes with as much freshness to the reader or audience first viewing the play as it does to characters in the play.

The naming of the flower girl is strangely at odds with this tactic. Apparently out of the blue, without introduction in the dialogue, Shaw starts calling her Liza when she enters the taxi. One might guess that he departed from his usual practice in order to signal a symbolic rite of passage: as she imaginatively shifts social spheres, she is no longer a mere flower girl. A comparison of our edition with the play's first edition, however, provides a more prosaic explanation. In the first edition, Liza not only remains "the flower girl" through the end of the act, but the act ends earlier. After declaring, "*I*'m going home in a taxi" and overcoming the cabby's resistance, she gives the directions to Angel Court, followed by, "Lets see how fast you can make her hop it." Whereupon "*she gets in and pulls the door to with a slam as the taxicab starts*," and the curtain falls with Freddy exclaiming, "Well, I'm dashed!" Absent are Freddy's "Goodbye," his raised hat, her "Bucknam Pellis," and all the business about her return home.

Since Shaw's unusual identification of Liza by name occurs at the point where he entered additions for the film, it was very likely a latter-day slip. In itself, the slip is a small matter (no more serious than Shaw's assigning the girl's speeches throughout the play to "Liza," whereas all characters call her "Eliza," as we will do), yet it introduces issues about our "definitive" edition. While the edition may be considered definitive because it is the author's latest, it presents a twofold problem: most specifically, we have a shift in mediums from the stage to film; more generally, we may question whether the talents of an author at 80 equal the talents of his prime.

Shaw retained bright sparks as a playwright into his ninety-fourth year yet sensed lessening powers in his last decades, and his revisions to *Pygmalion* offer one test of the durability of his genius. The film additions provide transitional passages less feasible for the stage yet useful for further character development, backgrounds, and action. Here our "definitive" version is valuable as it depicts Eliza's squalid living quarters, driving home a deprivation that contrasts strongly with the relative opulence of later scenes. And one would hardly want to omit other details added to the original—Freddy's dazed "Goodbye," the parallel with Higgins when he raises his hat, the flamboyant bravura of Eliza's "Bucknam Pellis," and her poignant exchange with the cabby. For all their signs of Shaw's resilient genius, however, most of the additions here lack the climactic theatrical snap, the surprise, delight, and zestful conclusiveness that trip the curtain in the act's original ending, leaving the audience to catch its breath. For a stage production, a happy compromise between the two versions might omit the taximan's lines and the drive home but include Freddy's raised hat and "Goodbye," with the curtain at "Bucknam Pellis." A director has to choose; the reader can have it both ways.

Whichever choice one makes, however, the act's dramatic richness evolves through the brilliant unfolding of its exposition, the sharpness of its characterizations, the liveliness of its interweaving themes, the range and clarity of its social depictions, the graphic illustration of its phonetic message, the economy and rapid pace of its action, and the bold fun with which it counterpoints mundane realities with flights of fantasy. Dramatically, Higgins's soapbox presentation of phonetics is the act's most impressive event, yet Eliza's plight gives his performance its fullest point. The act is especially important for showing her in her native element, in the hubbub of life but also on its edge, barely managing a pitiful existence. At the same time, Freddy, his mother, his sister, Pickering, the crowd, social stratifications, and numerous themes subtly anticipate and provide backgrounds for the rest of the play.

Remarkable over and above these elements is the fact that the act could stand by itself as a fully satisfying one-act play, with a well-constructed beginning, a dramatic and substantive middle, and, especially in its original stage version, a poignantly appealing end. As was true of its beginning, however, its end offers the beginning of the richer drama to come. It even introduces a new fantasy.

Without the concluding Angel Court scene, we have Eliza for the first time entering the magic of a taxi, en route to "Bucknam Pellis . . . where the King lives." Dramatically, the taxi offers a splendid visual climax at the curtain. Fancifully, Cinderella is delightfully modernized: the taxi amounts to Eliza's pumpkin turned into a golden carriage in

The church clock strikes the second quarter.

HIGGINS [*hearing in it the voice of God, rebuking him for his Pharisaic want of charity to the poor girl*] A reminder. [*He raises his hat solemnly; then throws a handful of money into the basket and follows Pickering*].

THE FLOWER GIRL [*picking up a half-crown*] Ah-ow-ooh! [*Picking up a couple of florins*] Aaah-ow-ooh! [*Picking up several coins*] Aaaaaah-ow-ooh! [*Picking up a half-sovereign*] Aaaaaaaaaaaaah-ow-ooh!!!

FREDDY [*springing out of a taxicab*] Got one at last. Hallo! [*To the girl*] Where are the two ladies that were here?

THE FLOWER GIRL. They walked to the bus when the rain stopped.

FREDDY. And left me with a cab on my hands! Damnation!

THE FLOWER GIRL [*with grandeur*] Never mind, young man. I'm going home in a taxi. [*She sails off to the cab. The driver puts his hand behind him and holds the door firmly shut against her. Quite understanding his mistrust, she shews him her handful of money*]. ~~Eightpence~~ A taxi fare aint no object to me, Charlie. [*He grins and opens the door*]. ~~Angel Court, Drury Lane, round the corner of Micklejohn's oil shop. Lets see how fast you can make her hop it.~~ [*~~She gets in and pulls the door to with a slam as the taxicab starts~~*]

~~FREDDY. Well, I'm dashed!~~

Here. What about the basket?

THE TAXIMAN. Give it here. Tuppence extra.

ELIZA. No: I don't want nobody to see it. [*She crushes it into the cab and gets in, continuing the conversation through the window*], Goodbye, Freddy.

FREDDY [*dazedly raising his hat*] Goodbye

TAXIMAN. Where to?

ELIZA. Bucknam Pellis [*Buckingham Palace*].

TAXIMAN What d'ye mean — Bucknam Pellis?

ELIZA. Don't you know where it is? In the Green Park, where the King lives. Goodbye, Freddy. Dont let me keep you standing there. Goodbye.

FREDDY. Goodbye. [*He goes*].

TAXIMAN. Here. What's this about Bucknam Pellis? What business have you at Bucknam Pellis?

ELIZA. Of course I havnt none. But I wasnt going to let him know that. You drive me home.

TAXIMAN. And wheres home?

ELIZA. Angel Court, Drury Lane, next Micklejohn's oil shop.

TAXIMAN. That sounds more like it, Judy. [*He drives off*].

Shaw's alterations to the end of act 1 for the 1938 film.

which she, now blessed by fortuitous wealth, will fly toward romantic splendor. With her return to Angel Court, on the other hand, Shaw graphically reminds us of grim realities that ground the dreams of would-be Cinderellas. Unlike the king's court, few angels bless this one. Yet now Eliza has a veritable surplus of *money*, an earthly key to the door of success that the phonetician has opened a crack—enough of a key, at least, to unlock thrilling dreams.

5

Act 2: Purgation

The setting and character description that launches act 2 will strike frequent readers of plays as unusually detailed. Indeed, Shaw was the first major English playwright to pay close attention to such matters. Once again we can perceive his early experience as a novelist, but once again his motives were primarily dramatic. As a theater critic in the 1890s, Shaw had suffered through hundreds of poorly staged plays. From tedious experience, he knew that faulty productions of negligible plays involved little loss, but faulty productions of fine ones could result in artistic sacrilege. For example, directors often hacked up plays by Shakespeare to save time, highlight star actors, or indulge their own dubious tastes. To avoid such mishaps, Shaw frequently supervised the casting and directing of his plays, as he did with *Pygmalion* in London. Yet *Pygmalion* had premiered in Vienna, and the more widely his dramas were performed, the fewer productions he could supervise personally. Stage and character directions offered an answer. Besides serving readers, they could cue directors and actors about the effects he desired.

Details here are a case in point. The drawing room, Higgins's primary living area, reflects a workaholic who draws few distinctions between his profession and his leisure. Double doors in the center of the back wall highlight characters' entrances and exits. Shaw's description leads one through these doors and into the room from the actors' (or visitors') point of view: file cabinets and numerous phonetics instruments are to the right, with an easy chair and a fireplace beyond them (toward the audience). To the left is a cabinet of shallow drawers topped by a telephone, and occupying most of the side wall is a grand piano. Much as the scientific paraphernalia serves Higgins's profession, so do the telephone and piano, whose bench *"for the players"* (not just one) extends the full length of the keyboard, allowing the professor and his students to explore a broad range of tone, pitch, and inflection in speech (33–34).[1]

The striking of a clock on the mantelpiece will become metaphoric at the start of act 4. *"A dessert dish heaped with fruit and sweets, mostly chocolates,"* seemingly incidental, will prove metaphoric as well. Engravings on the walls, *"mostly Piranesis and mezzotint portraits. No paintings,"* suggest Higgins's relationship to Ovid's Pygmalion. Piranesi, a great etcher of classical architecture, was popular for his scenes of Roman and Greek antiquities and for hauntingly fanciful plates titled "Imaginary Prisons." His neoclassical engravings reveal a consummate technician, while the boldness, drama, and surrealism of his fantasies amount to architectural poetry.

Thus, Higgins's drawing room characterizes the man. In contrast to Pickering, who appears in act 1 merely as *"an elderly gentleman of the amiable military type,"* a description sufficient for his role as a foil, the room's resident has a compulsive, explosive temperament. His professional gear befits an *"energetic, scientific type, heartily, even violently interested in everything that can be studied as a scientific object."* His telephone befits his business and communication skills; his grand piano befits his scientific and cultural interests, both susceptible to stormy noise; and Piranesi's precise, classical engravings befit his exacting, austere nature, one capable of bizarre, imaginative flights. Giving intimate twists to these, we have an individual of 40 or thereabouts who is, *"but for his years and size, rather like a very impetuous baby . . . and requiring almost as much watching to keep him out of unintended mischief,"* one who varies from *"genial bullying . . . to stormy petulance . . . so entirely frank and void of malice that he remains likeable even in his least reasonable moments."*

Much as act 1 opens with a post-theater ending, act 2 starts with Higgins closing the last of his file drawers, commenting to Pickering, "Well, I think thats the whole show." Since it is 11:00 A.M. and Higgins's phonetics would involve many acts, Pickering must have had an intensive morning. "Done up," he rapidly confirms his host's expertise (to the audience) by declaring that, while he has fancied himself because he can pronounce 24 vowel sounds, Higgins's 130 utterly beat him. When Higgins chuckles and goes to the piano to eat sweets, we glimpse the child briefly, an impression that suddenly shifts when Mrs. Pearce, his housekeeper, hesitantly announces a young, very common woman. Hearing that her accent is "something dreadful," the obsessive professional rushes for a phonograph cylinder, explaining to Pickering that he will write her speech phonetically, "and then we'll get her on the phonograph so that you can turn her on as often as you like with the written transcript before you" (36).

Higgins has unwittingly given himself away. He means, "we'll *record* her *voice* [not 'get her'] on the phonograph so that you can turn her *accent* [not 'her'] on as often as you like." Instead, he converts a human being into a subject and object at the same time, an accent to be caught in a machine that one can turn on and off at will. Her humanity is unimportant, even a nuisance. And, at first, a damned nuisance it seems to be.

Almost literally damned. Dramatically framed by the double doorway, the flower girl enters *"in state"* (an echo of "Bucknam Pellis"), her majesty including a hat with three brightly dyed ostrich feathers, a nearly clean apron, and a shoddy coat, slightly tidied. While the pathos, innocent vanity, and consequential air of this deplorable figure touch Pickering, the petulant baby in Higgins makes an intolerable grievance of his disappointment, reducing her to a phonetic scribble: "This is the girl I jotted down last night. She's no use." He has records of the "Lisson Grove lingo": "Be off with you" (36–37). Except for God's intercession, she was hardly worth a few coins in act 1. Now she's not worth a cylinder.

Act 2: Purgation

Like a lost soul who has witlessly stepped into hell, the poor creature is unaware of peril. Girded by her royal entry, her new wealth, her vanity, her spunky commercial spirit, and a Mission, the girl stands her ground. She may not be the Queen of Sheba, *but*—she turns to Mrs. Pearce: "Did you tell him I come in a taxi?"

This query heralds a host of confusions about gentility and the value of money that separate the girl from the upper classes. Clearly, all she can know is her own integrity, the value of money to her, and what she has seen or heard from the gutter about ladies and gentlemen. And clearly this is not nearly enough for a gentleman's drawing room, but more than enough for Shaw, who propels the scene with great virtuosity through a comedy of contrasts, dislocations, inversions, shifts, twists, turns, and pathos that explore the immense gaps between her perceptions and the realities of Higgins, Pickering, and Mrs. Pearce, starting with Mrs. Pearce's response: "Nonsense, girl! what do you think a gentleman like Mr Higgins cares what you came in?" (37–38).

Pooh-pooh to the mystique of taxis, a matter so momentous to a flower girl, so trivial to gentlefolk? Not so. The girl deflects Mrs. Pearce's incredible question, turning the social situation topsy-turvy by putting her down on grounds of snobbery, then putting down Higgins on grounds of economics: "Oh, we *are* proud! He aint above giving lessons, not him: I heard him say so. Well, I aint come here to ask for any compliment [as though one might be offered]; and if my money's not good enough I can go elsewhere. . . . Now you know, dont you? I'm coming to have lessons, I am." So far as she is concerned, Higgins is a vendor, she a customer. For once, the professor is nearly speechless: "Well!!! . . . What do you expect me to say to you?" The lady condescends to his breathless cue: "Well, if you was a gentleman you might ask me to sit down, I think. Dont I tell you I'm bringing you business?" Thus, the lady confirms her dignity and place and even teaches this male some manners, much as she had done with the mother at the start of act 1. But then she was below. Now she is on top. For an instant.

Higgins responds with his customary gentility: "Pickering: shall we ask this baggage to sit down, or shall we throw her out of the window?" In the flash of a nightmare or fairy tale, the gentleman in his drawing room becomes a Monster in his den and she a terrified animal running to the piano, "*where she turns at bay*," uttering one of her howls. Could the devil be more ominous to a soul in darkness? "*Wounded and whimpering*," she tries to regain her dignity: "I wont be called a baggage when Ive offered to pay like any lady." The men stare at her, amazed.

Like a good angel, Pickering breaks the impasse gently. Not presuming to humiliate this pathetic creature by questioning her ladyship, he asks, "But what is it that you want?" Notably, his kindness, not Higgins's brutality, elicits the truth: "I want to be a lady in a flower shop. . . . But they wont take me unless I can talk more genteel. He said he could teach me." Her plight is simply a version of those ambitious young men with lower-class accents she had heard Higgins talk about in act 1. Mrs. Pearce draws a bottom line unkindly but accurately: "How can you be such a foolish ignorant girl as to think you could afford to pay Mr Higgins?" Still, as in the girl's gutter existence, money appears to turn the trick and return the monster to his senses, asking "How much?"

She comes back, grasping victory from the jaws of defeat: how inconceivable that his charity the night before came from above, from his fancying he heard God's voice in the quarter-hour (not even the full-hour) striking of St. Paul's clock. Obviously, it came from below. Anyone who would throw away such a fortune must have been tipsy.

Despite this natural misapprehension, however, she has indeed managed a small triumph. Instead of throwing her out the window, Higgins commands her to sit down (which is what she had suggested):

THE FLOWER GIRL. Oh, if youre going to make a compliment of it—

HIGGINS [*thundering at her*] Sit down.

MRS PEARCE [*severely*] Sit down, girl. Do as youre told.

THE FLOWER GIRL. Ah-ah-ah-ow-ow-oo! [*She stands, half rebellious, half bewildered*].

Act 2: Purgation

PICKERING [*very courteous*] Wont you sit down? . . .

LIZA [*coyly*] Dont mind if I do. [*She sits down.*] (39)

This exchange characterizes the four speakers sparely and precisely: Higgins is brusque at one moment, stormy the next; the flower girl shifts from an imagined compliment to her native howl to mimicking gentility; the class-conscious, no-nonsense Mrs. Pearce exercises her authority, seconding her employer; the ever-courteous Pickering draws no class distinctions. Tonally, Higgins approximates a baritone, Eliza a soprano, Mrs. Pearce an alto, and Pickering a bass-baritone. The lower tonality of Mrs. Pearce and Pickering matches their relative stability throughout the scene, while Higgins and Eliza run a gamut of emotional extremes.

Once again, Pickering's tactfulness bridges a strategic gap, defusing the flower girl's rebelliousness and bewilderment so that she gives her name to Higgins and the audience. But her uttering "Liza Doolittle" trips another switch, prompting the men to spring into a ditty on variants of her name—Eliza, Elizabeth, Betsy, and Bess. Disparaging their fun and laughter as "silly," Eliza calls their card but misses its trick. In act 1, her laughter at Higgins's mimicking her howl threw off her intimidation, sparking her attention to his boast that he could make a lady of her. Now Shaw uses the men's laughter to spark a new mood in Higgins, one that moves him rapidly and naturally toward one of the play's most crucial decisions. Relaxed by humor, Higgins actually listens closely to her explanation that since a lady friend of hers gets French lessons for 18 pence an hour, and he will only be teaching her her own language, she won't give him more than a shilling: "Take it or leave it."

Engaged now, "*rattling his keys and his cash in his pockets*" (keys to his way of life, along with the cash supporting it), Higgins calculates fancifully that, on a percentage basis, a shilling of the girl's income would equal £60 for a millionaire—an extravagant sum for a lesson. His striking comparison, not her character or plight, grips him. Yet in voicing a cash equivalent, he illuminates an extraordinary aspect of Eliza's character. Of all the ways she might have chosen to spend his money, she has pursued perhaps the most practical, intelligent, imaginative, farsighted one, seeking out the only person she knows who might make her dreams possible, the man who declared that her curbstone English would keep her in the gutter to the end of her days and who boasted that with his teaching she could pass as a duchess or a shop assistant. Fulfillment of the latter, more realistic ambition, and perhaps of her life, rests precariously in him, yet now he baffles her notions of gentility and mentions £60 a lesson.

When Eliza, terrified and jangled, weeps, "But I aint got sixty pounds," and Higgins gives her his silk handkerchief, instructing her to use it, not her sleeve, "if you wish to become a lady in a shop," he inadvertently takes another step. After tossing her the change, this is his second gift, and he couches it in terms of teaching and her ambition. All it takes for the most fateful step now is for Pickering to recall Higgins's Covent Garden boast and to bet all the expenses of her training that Higgins can't do it. Having evolved from the spontaneous jocularity of jingling her name to jingling cash in his pockets and comparing her offer of payment with a millionaire's, Higgins has primed himself for the temptation of this ultimate challenge: "She's so deliciously low—so horribly dirty—" (40). Carried away like a mad scientist, a daring gambler, or a child, he orders Mrs. Pearce to clean her, with Monkey Brand (a harsh cleanser) if necessary, to wallop her if necessary, to house her in the dustbin.

Shaw gives comic zest to this fanatical exuberance over the next ten minutes by developing it in gusts and counterpointing it with resistance, admonitions, and cautions from Mrs. Pearce, complaints and self-righteous assertions from Eliza, and amusement from Pickering. To Eliza's complaint over his command that her clothes be taken off and burned, Higgins responds, "We want none of your Lisson Grove prudery here, young woman. Youve got to learn to behave like a duchess" (41). To the chiming of Pickering and Mrs. Pearce that he be reasonable, his hurricane becomes a zephyr of amiable surprise and charitable reason: "All I propose is that we should be kind to this poor girl. We must help her to prepare and fit herself for her new station in life." When Mrs. Pearce warns that the girl may be married and Eliza exclaims, "Garn!" he exclaims, "Married indeed! Dont you know that a woman of that class looks a worn out drudge of fifty a year after she's married?" (42). After Eliza then asks, "Whood marry me?" he rhapsodizes, "By George, Eliza, the streets will be strewn with the bodies of men shooting themselves for your sake before Ive done with you." Taking this seriously, Eliza declares, "I'm going away. He's off his chump," whereupon he keeps her there by telling Mrs. Pearce, "You neednt order the new clothes for her. Throw her out." When Mrs. Pearce advises her to go home to her parents and Eliza explains that she has none—that her sixth stepmother turned her out—he proclaims territorial rights: "The girl doesnt belong to anybody—is no use to anybody but me" (43).

In the midst of this whirlwind, Eliza's plight becomes increasingly clear. Thrown out by her parents, scraping by on her own, unlikely to be married except at her peril, her prospects are bleak, except for Higgins. Yet what a troubling savior he is. At Higgins's assertion that she would only drink if she had money, she declares, "Oh you are a brute. It's a lie." She appeals to Pickering, because "youre a gentleman," whereupon Pickering asks, "Does it occur to you, Higgins, that the girl has some feelings?" The professor's response waves warning flags:

HIGGINS [*looking critically at her*] Oh no, I dont think so. Not any feelings that we need bother about. [*Cheerily*] Have you, Eliza?

LIZA. I got my feelings same as anyone else.

HIGGINS [*to Pickering, reflectively*] You see the difficulty?

PICKERING. Eh? What difficulty?

HIGGINS. To get her to talk grammar. The mere pronunciation is easy enough.

LIZA. I dont want to talk grammar. I want to talk like a lady in a flower-shop. (43–44)

This exchange epitomizes Higgins's instinct to look at Eliza as a scientific subject, not a human being, while her response reveals a human being who counters his insularity and quickly picks up the idea of her feelings. Pickering has given her a fresh frame of reference. In not noticing how readily she adopts it, Higgins shows that his ear can be less sharp than hers. Not listening to what she says, he hears only how she says it, missing the fact that his deafness to her humanity is the greatest "difficulty." As a final twist, Eliza's insistence that she does not want to talk grammar resembles the humor of Molière's Bourgeois Gentleman, who is utterly delighted when he hears that he has been speaking prose all his life. A more profound difficulty than her lack of grammar, Shaw suggests with a smile, is her lack of common cultural denominators.

The quality of Mrs. Pearce's opposition to her employer, meanwhile, demonstrates Shaw's effectiveness in rounding out supporting roles. The housekeeper's class-consciousness and brusqueness toward Eliza reflect the historical and social fact that, of all persons in a genteel household, servants were the most likely to be sensitive to matters of class because they had close contacts with the upper classes and roots in the lower ones. Well-established ladies and gentlemen could afford to be easygoing about such matters because no one questioned their place, whereas distinctions of "place" gave a servant status. For Mrs. Pearce, Eliza is simply out of place as a visitor or client in Mr. Higgins's drawing room. To indulge her employer's professional quirks, she compromises propriety in admitting Eliza, then finds that she must make the girl know her place. More revealing of Mrs. Pearce's character, however, are her concerns about Higgins's plans to bring Eliza into the household. This bothers her less for his sake or her own than for Eliza's. Since Higgins falls below his place—his responsibilities to the girl—she rises above hers in the girl's defense: "You cant walk over everybody like this. . . . Nonsense, sir. You mustnt talk like that to her. . . . Stop, Mr Higgins. I wont allow it. It's you that are wicked" (41–43).

Most important, Mrs. Pearce introduces a concern that will climax traumatically in act 4. She worries about Eliza's future, repeating her point as she tries to drive it home to Higgins (and the audience): "But what's to become of her? . . . Do be sensible, sir."

> MRS PEARCE. . . . And what is to become of her when youve finished your teaching? You must look ahead a little.

> HIGGINS [*impatiently*] Whats to become of her if I leave her in the gutter? Tell me that, Mrs Pearce.

> MRS PEARCE. Thats her own business, not yours, Mr Higgins.

> HIGGINS. Well, when Ive done with her, we can throw her back into the gutter; and then it will be her own business again. . . .

> LIZA. Oh, youve no feeling heart in you: you dont care for nothing but yourself. (43–44)

Eliza's sentiment rises both from Mrs. Pearce's spirited defense of her and from the articulation of feeling she has just acquired from Pickering. Higgins brushes past personal or social or moral impediments. He is in the grip of his science, his religion, his childishness, his challenge. He indeed cares for little but himself. On behalf of his cause, he is a monster of pride.

The monster in Higgins first surfaces in act 1 when he seems like the Law, a magician, and a demigod, all in one. In act 2 the monster reemerges, not just when Eliza first perceives him as such but more pointedly when, "*tempted*" by Pickering's bet, he orders her clothes taken off and burned, prompting her to cry, "Youre no gentleman, youre not, to talk of such things. I'm a good girl, I am; and I know what the like of you are, I do." What are his "like"? What kind of man would Mrs. Pearce call "wicked" for tempting Eliza with beautiful dresses and gentility? What kind of man does Eliza suddenly suspect when, his eyes "*beginning to twinkle with mischief*," he offers her chocolates, causing her to halt: "How do I know what might be in them? Ive heard of girls being drugged by the like of you." When Mrs. Pearce objects, "Mr Higgins: youre tempting the girl. It's not right. She should think of the future," what kind of man would cunningly respond: "At her age! Nonsense! Time enough to think of the future when you havnt any future to think of. No, Eliza: do as this lady does: think of other people's futures; but never think of your own. Think of chocolates, and taxis, and gold, and diamonds." Perceiving that chocolates and taxis are one thing and gold and diamonds quite another, Eliza draws a line: "No: I dont want no gold and no diamonds. I'm a good girl, I am" (40–45).

While this line resembles many that Eliza drew in act 1, it extends them. There, she upheld her virtue against society's assumption that those who sell flowers from the gutter often sell themselves as well. Here, she confronts what she perceives as an immediate threat to her virtue by a creature—no gentleman but a wolf in genteel clothing—who seeks to tempt and overwhelm her in his lair. Like Little Red Riding Hood, she may be gobbled up by this wily beast. If she could read more adult warnings, she might also have found his type in Samuel Richardson's novel *Pamela, or Virtue Rewarded* (1740), where a lustful young squire pants after a virtuous serving girl for hundreds of pages. Scores of melodramas had made the type infamous, even to flower girls, and what books, the theater, and legends did not tell them, they learned sordidly on the streets. To Eliza, Higgins personifies all of these, even back to a frightening source: against her Virtue, here is a Tempter replete with pride and perversity in his weird den, seeking to seduce her with worldly luxuries.

Shaw dramatizes this echo of a diabolical archetype by having Higgins driven, by Satan's sin of pride, to undertake the audacious experiment, then by portraying his fervor through shifts that range from imperiousness and threats to duplicitous kindness, extravagant fancies, coaxing rationalizations, and a deceptive pledge of good faith in sharing a chocolate with Eliza, all couched in a web of increasing temptations aimed at snaring a poor virgin whose personal ends he subverts to his own. Against this demonic vivacity and variety, Mrs. Pearce acts as a good angel even more than Pickering. Yet the good angel loses the battle: Eliza repeatedly threatens to leave but does not. The temptations are too tantalizing.

Act 2: Purgation

From Higgins's point of view, such melodrama is nonsense, but to entice Eliza he pulls out the stops of his rhetorical organ. The door to his climax opens when Pickering at last seconds Mrs. Pearce, admonishing him that Eliza "must understand thoroughly what she's doing," and then addresses her as "Miss Doolittle." Hearing this remarkable respect for the first time in her life and overwhelmed by it, she utters another of her howls, setting Higgins off: "There! Thats all youll get out of Eliza. Ah-ah-ow-oo! No use explaining. As a military man you ought to know that. Give her her orders: thats enough for her. Eliza: you are to live here for the next six months, learning how to speak beautifully, like a lady in a florist's shop. If youre good and do whatever youre told, you shall sleep in a proper bedroom, and have lots to eat, and money to buy chocolates and take rides in taxis." This answers to Pickering's military background, to his own ends, to Eliza's dreams. "If youre naughty and idle you will sleep in the back kitchen among the black beetles, and be walloped by Mrs Pearce with a broomstick." Here, military discipline and a touch of Cinderella combine, with the strict Mrs. Pearce playing the role of Cinderella's—and Eliza's—stepmother. "At the end of six months you shall go to Buckingham Palace in a carriage, beautifully dressed." Echoing the link between Eliza and Cinderella in act 1, this sets the fairy-tale fantasy sparkling with fine clothing, a real carriage, a resplendent dream. "If the King finds out youre not a lady, you will be taken by the police to the Tower of London, where your head will be cut off as a warning to other presumptuous flower girls." This threat of doom for failure draws upon Eliza's fear of the police in act 1, here hugely shadowed by ghosts of Henry VIII and Bluebeard. "If you are not found out, you shall have a present of seven-and-sixpence to start life with as a lady in a shop." Now he returns to Eliza's original ambition and budgeting, linking these with her assumption that this would be the real start of her life. "If you refuse this offer you will be a most ungrateful wicked girl; and the angels will weep for you." At last he circles back to ground zero, giving Eliza's choice a moral and spiritual dimension, attended by a heavenly host (45–46).

Higgins's conclusion—"Now are you satisfied, Pickering? . . . Can I put it more plainly and fairly, Mrs Pearce?"—comes as a comic coda to his extravagant aria. Oddly yet aptly, despite its absurdity, Higgins's fanciful flight reflects his evolution in this scene. On the one hand, it appeals, in a fairy-tale fashion, to Eliza's ambition and dreams. On the other hand, its comic circuit displays Higgins's realism and capacity for dreaming. Realistically, he desires to snare Eliza for his experiment; imaginatively, the experiment challenges him with a great test of the interests and talents that lie at the core of his life, a fantastic, creative test through which he, like Pygmalion, may realize *his* ambition and dreams through his Galatea. Thus he and Eliza, so diverse in their viewpoints and sophistication, may join for an equally significant time in their lives.

Led away by Mrs. Pearce, who, at last capitulating, commands, "Dont answer back, girl. You dont understand the gentleman," Eliza continues to bleat her refrains, "I always been a good girl. . . . I have my feelings the same as anyone else" (46), but she goes. Realities and fantasies are coalescing.

*   *   *

At this point, one can reconstruct Shaw's original text by skipping three pages from *"Mrs Pearce shuts the the door; and Eliza's plaints are no longer audible"* (46) to *"Pickering has come from the hearth to the chair and seated himself astride of it with his arms on the back to cross-examine [Higgins]"* (49), and then altering this last to *"Pickering comes from the hearth to the chair and sits astride it with his arms on the back."* Two things may be noticed in such a scan. First, the original version is less wordy than the revision and describes Pickering's action in the active voice, while the revised version uses the passive voice. Second, the original version moves rapidly from the dynamics of Eliza's plaints as she is led off to Pickering's brief cross-examining. For those with a keen eye and dramatic sensibility, these differences may capsulize the greater energy and pace of the stage version as opposed to much of the screen adaptation.

The bedroom-bathroom vignette added for the film, like the film's ending for act 1, has value because it provides extra glimpses of Eliza. Here, we have her prudishness and her unfamiliarity with personal hygiene and upper-class ways comically rendered as Mrs. Pearce prepares to bathe her—and finally does, even as Eliza screams. The dialogue, however, has less spark than most of the play and seems slightly askew from the overall characterizations of these two. For example, Eliza lacks her earlier feistiness, vanity, and sense of personal mission when she remarks, "O-h, I couldnt sleep here, missus. It's too good for the likes of me. I should be afraid to touch anything. I aint a duchess yet, you know." And Mrs. Pearce adopts more of a mission and even less tact than elsewhere when she says, "I want to change you from a frowzy slut to a clean respectable girl" (47, 48). The different key may be defended as a portrayal of the women as they are when out of the gentlemen's sight. It also serves to bond them in a specific way, and Eliza's physical purgation offers a memorable moment. Yet most of this effect is implicit or explicit elsewhere, and because the scene is not easy to mount and arrests the play's action, stage productions commonly omit it.

*   *   *

Shaw removes Eliza from the stage not just because she needs a bath but for the dramatic purpose of having Pickering ask Higgins if he is a man of good character where women are concerned. This exchange develops Pickering as Eliza's kindly protector, clears up the sexual innuendos that she has introduced in the preceding dialogue, allows for Higgins's revelation of his antiromantic nature, and backgrounds the following scene with Eliza's father, all of which permits a realistic sense of passing time before Eliza returns. And even more important, Higgins's response intimately, economically, and almost diagrammatically anticipates his personal relations with Eliza at crucial points later in the play: "I find that the moment I let myself make friends with a woman, I become selfish and tyrannical. Women upset everything. When you let them into your life, you find that the woman is driving at one thing and youre driving at another. . . . I suppose the woman wants to live her own life; and the man wants to live his; and each tries to drag the other on to the wrong track" (50).

Right now, Higgins's track is simply science, prompting him to call Eliza "that thing" and to assert his confirmed bachelorhood. Shaw seems already set on puncturing romantic notions. But what can one do with sentimentalists in the audience who know that what men deny they often fall prey to? Well, one can call in reinforcements. Thus, Shaw returns Mrs. Pearce and prepares again for the comic climax of act 3 by having her urge Higgins to mind his swearing and manners before the girl. He must set her a good example. Only that morning he applied a word beginning with *b* (*bloody*) to his boots, the butter, and brown bread. The professor begs off on grounds of alliteration, "natural to a poet," but she then seizes this rare chance to nag him like a mother hen about his dress and table manners. Upon her suggestion that he not wipe his fingers on his dressing gown when he eats, he yells, "Oh very well, very well: I'll wipe them in my hair in future," after which he describes himself to Pickering as "a shy, diffident sort of man," never able to feel grown up, and expresses surprise that Mrs. Pearce thinks him arbitrary, overbearing, bossy (50–52).

By this scene, Higgins's comic appeal as a bundle of extremes that rapidly, variably, and capriciously play against one another has been roundly introduced. Within moments, he shifts between extraordinary intelligence and remarkable ignorance, sophistication and naïveté, reasoning adult and impetuous child, personal cunning and social ineptitude, realities and fantasies, worldliness and spirituality, selfishness and charity, obstreperousness and pacification, insularity and sensitivity, tyranny and democracy, sourness and sweetness, rage and good humor, irony and farce. While he is obsessively scientific, his obsession makes his science an art, an exacting, creative, social, even spiritual pursuit. On the one hand, he takes to science like a dynamo, embodying the comedy of man-as-machine, as famously perceived by Henri Bergson, yet on the other hand, his contradictions make him humanly comic, according to the comedy of character as defined by George Meredith.[2]

When Mrs. Pearce now returns apprehensively with the news that a "dustman" (trash collector), Alfred Doolittle, has come about his daughter, the child in Higgins vanishes and the canny, aggressive adult and scientist in him instantly join hands: "Send the blackguard up." Pickering fears trouble, but Higgins responds, "Oh no: I think not. If theres any trouble he shall have it with me, not I with him. And we are sure to get something interesting out of him."—"About the girl?"—

Act 2: Purgation

"No. I mean his dialect" (53).

The dustman receives his first comeuppance when Mrs. Pearce, not deigning a "Mister," announces him merely as "Doolittle, sir." With the melodramatic pose of a father whose honor has been wounded, Doolittle menacingly declares that he wants his daughter, only to have Higgins explode his show. Punning on "kept" woman, the professor calls his bluff by commanding, "Take her away. Do you suppose I'm going to keep your daughter for you?" and out-acts the dustman by going to the telephone to call the police for attempted extortion. Yet Doolittle proves as variable as Higgins. Like his daughter, his pretense has been undercut, but he is relatively invulnerable because he has little vanity and does not believe his pretense. Without the honor she prizes, he can shift around it, and unlike her, he is highly articulate. He now momentarily disarms the hard-nosed phonetician by imploring sweetly, "Be human, Governor," and by defending himself with an eloquence that fascinates the rhetorician in Higgins: "Pickering: this chap has a certain natural gift of rhetoric. Observe the rhythm of his native woodnotes wild. . . . Sentimental rhetoric! thats the Welsh strain in him. It also accounts for his mendacity and dishonesty" (53–55).

Typical of Shaw's capacity for highly condensed wit, this last takes only four short sentences to bristle with Shavian fireworks. Higgins's sensitivity to Doolittle's rhetoric reveals the sharp-eared professional. His sensitivity to Doolittle's rhythm reveals the poet in the professional. His reference to "native woodnotes wild" reveals the Miltonist and playfully sophisticated ironist as he makes a point colorfully by alluding to Milton's "L'Allegro," which speaks of "sweetest Shakespeare, fancy's child," warbling "his native wood-notes wild." Thus, Doolittle, who has implored *sweetly* and just spoken in a manner *most musical, most melancholy* (a line Shaw lifts from Milton's "Il Penseroso"), is satirically linked to the Bard, whose "word music" Shaw much admired. The satire cuts two ways (or three, if one includes Milton), reverberating between Shakespeare and Doolittle, who would seem to be closest to the rustic implied beautifully (and satirically here) by "native woodnotes wild." The satire delivers another cut when Higgins identifies such rhetoric as sentimental, then another when the professional in him links it to Doolittle's Welsh strain, and yet another when he relates the rhetoric (and the Welsh strain?) to mendacity and dishonesty.

Eliza's insistence on being a "good girl" and Mrs. Pearce's recommendation that she return to her parents are thrust into startling new lights when Doolittle soon assumes that her fate is highly favorable: "Heres a career opening for her as you might say" (56). Above a flower girl and a streetwalker, the relatively secure status and steady employment of a kept woman—for not just one but two gentlemen—should offer Eliza the best career option she could possibly hope for.

Finally the issue Doolittle introduces boils down to the realities of economics versus society's presumptions about morality. A little background on the issue may clarify Shaw's irreverent treatment of it here. In his preface to *Major Barbara* years before, Shaw had boldly advanced an economic argument that relates to Eliza and her father. There, he argues that Sunday school platitudes based on "blessed are the poor" obscure the fact that the greatest of all evils is poverty, because poverty breeds weakness, ignorance, disease, malnutrition, slums, prostitution, crime, and a host of other social ills. Society, Shaw observed, gets its conscience off the hook by punishing crimes that derive from poverty, or by tolerating poverty "as if it were either a wholesome tonic for lazy people or else a virtue to be embraced as St Francis embraced it. If a man is indolent, let him be poor. If he is drunken, let him be poor. If he is not a gentleman, let him be poor. If he is addicted to the fine arts or to pure science instead of to trade and finance, let him be poor. . . . Let nothing be done for 'the undeserving': let him be poor."[3] Such self-righteousness backfires, however, since the "undeserving" will always be with us, breeding the evils of poverty.

Later, in a statement opposing stage censorship, Shaw was equally revolutionary. Declaring himself "a specialist in immoral and heretical plays," he explained: "My reputation has been gained by my persistent struggle to force the public to reconsider its morals. In particular, I regard much current morality as to economic and sexual relations as disastrously wrong." What is morality? As society applies it, it is no absolute or divine standard, though society may pretend that it is. In practice, rather, it is social consensus. Thus, "whatever is contrary to established manners and customs is immoral. An immoral act or doctrine is not necessarily a sinful one: on the contrary, every advance in thought and conduct is by definition immoral until it has converted the majority."[4]

In many of his plays, Shaw inserts a character who diverts the action in disconcerting, often amusing ways. Doolittle, a strong example of such a one, extends and twists Shaw's ideas on poverty and morality. Declaring that "all I ask is my rights as a father; and youre the last man alive to expect me to let her go for nothing," he asks Higgins, "Well, whats a five-pound note to you? and whats Eliza to me?" At the start of his posing, he sat down *"magisterially"* to little success; now he sits down, like Solomon, *"judicially"*:

PICKERING. I think you ought to know, Doolittle, that Mr Higgins's intentions are entirely honorable.

DOOLITTLE. Course they are, Governor. If I thought they wasn't, I'd ask fifty.

HIGGINS [*revolted*] Do you mean to say that you would sell your daughter for £50? . . .

PICKERING. Have you no morals, man?

DOOLITTLE [*unabashed*] Cant afford them, Governor. Neither could you if you was as poor as me. . . .

HIGGINS [*troubled*] I dont know what to do, Pickering. There can be no question that as a matter of morals it's a positive crime to give this chap a farthing. And yet I feel a sort of rough justice in his claim.

DOOLITTLE. Thats it, Governor. Thats all I say. A father's heart, as it were.

PICKERING. Well, I know the feeling; but really it seems hardly right— (57–58)

This dialogue takes its most bizarre turn in Doolittle's declaration that he cannot afford morals. Are morals just an option of privileged classes? Money, we know, can cause morals to somersault on Wall Street, in government, business, or divorces, or in dividing Aunt Prunella's estate. Doolittle overstates his case, yet he raises the idea that the poor can afford some morals far less than the rich can, and to that degree at least, morals are a relative matter. Eliza, one must notice, does maintain morals, choosing to be "a good girl" at whatever cost, yet she imperils her future by doing so. For her, the cost is far dearer—and her virtue proportionately greater—than it would be were she a woman of wealth.

Such relativities trouble Higgins, rousing his feeling (showing that he has some) of a rough justice in Doolittle's claim. Still, Shaw couches the claim in irony and hypocrisy: Doolittle asserts "the rights of a father" and "a father's heart." These platitudes offer a lower-class view of the common Victorian practice of arranged marriages, of daughters being "sold" into marriage by their fathers and mothers on the basis of the groom's wealth. Doolittle may have this custom in the back of his fertile mind, since shortly afterward he advises Higgins to "marry Eliza while she's young and dont know no better" (60). A final irony, another of Shaw's codas, appears in Pickering's response to the "father's heart." Good-heartedly not recognizing Doolittle's hypocrisy, he accepts his "feeling" but finds the whole matter hardly right, which indeed it hardly is.

Shaw has Doolittle counter Pickering's doubt with an audaciously original case for the "undeserving poor," among whom he frankly places himself: "Think of what that means to a man. It means that he's up agen middle class morality all the time," and that means that he is denied finances because he is "undeserving," even though his needs and appetites exceed a deserving man's. "What is middle class morality? Just an excuse for never giving me anything. Therefore, I ask you, as two gentlemen, not to play that game on me. I'm playing straight with you. I aint pretending to be deserving. I'm undeserving; and I mean to go on being undeserving. I like it; and thats the truth" (58).

Doolittle's case reflects Shaw's version of it in *Major Barbara*. What it lacks in not presenting Shaw's framework, it makes up for as a dramatic example. If one gives credence to Shaw's argument, one must be prepared, on behalf of society's well-being, to swallow its real-life Doolittles, who, so aptly named, do little. The personality, rhetoric, and humor of the dustman make his case partially palatable, especially when he cites the middle-class "game" of moral self-righteousness. In argument if not in deed, his game is relatively straight, though his father's heart is a joker, and he plays his cards with the right gentlemen. After all, Higgins's identification of people's origins resembles a game, and he tackles his profession with the ardor of a gamester. Then, too, Pickering's bet and their plans for Eliza amount to a demanding, ingenious game.

Doolittle's native rhetorical powers suggest yet another game to Higgins: "Pickering: if we were to take this man in hand for three months, he could choose between a seat in the Cabinet and a popular pulpit in Wales." This is at least half-serious. What can serve a politician or preacher more powerfully than a mastery of public speaking? Doolittle puts down such temptations in a wit that naturally puns with "game" and "line": "I'm a thinking man and game for politics or religion or social reform same as all the other amusements, [but] it's a dog's life. . . . Undeserving poverty is my line."

His game and line have been so successful with Higgins that £5 is forthcoming. Pickering fears that "he'll make bad use of it." Doolittle's response presents a brilliant summary of his case, temperament, and economic canniness. All of these contrast sharply with Eliza's prudent use of money, suggesting that while her course may be upward, his will remain forever the same: "Not me, Governor, so help me I wont. Dont you be afraid that I'll save it and spare it and live idle on it. There wont be a penny of it left by Monday. I'll have to go to work same as if I'd never had it. It wont pauperize me, you bet. Just one good spree for myself and the missus, giving pleasure to ourselves and employment to others, and satisfaction to you to think it's not been throwed away. You couldnt spend it better" (59).

When Higgins finds this brilliance irresistible and offers him £10, Doolittle shows remarkable integrity in his hedonistic principles by declining it. It might tempt him, or at least his mate, toward middle-class morality: "She wouldnt have the heart to spend ten. . . . Ten pounds is a lot of money: it makes a man feel prudent like; and then goodbye to happiness." Trying ultimately to salvage some morality from this dusky business, Pickering asks, "Why dont you marry that missus of yours?" Doolittle's reply produces a final comic twist: *He* is willing, but she is not. Without marriage, he is a slave to her, having to be agreeable, give her presents, and buy her clothes to no end. On these grounds, man to man, he advises Higgins to marry Eliza—not for morality's sake, but to be free from the personal and economic burdens of pleasing a mistress. Thus, a heartfelt inversion concludes the scene's comedy of inversions, perversity, and originality. The untenable has become tenuously tenable through characters and a situation that turn melodrama and conventional attitudes about morality, poverty, and privilege on their heads.

The Eliza who appears (framed in the central doorway once again) when Doolittle opens the door on his way out is an artful predecessor of the heroines in silly films who are suddenly transformed from dowdies to beauties when their glasses are removed, hair restyled, makeup redone, and clothing glamorized to produce Hollywood's version of an acceptable princess. Although dainty and exquisitely clean in a simple cotton kimono from Higgins's travels, she immediately reveals her gutter origins in her "Garn!" to her father and her "Dont I look silly?" to all present. To improve herself in her own eyes (but actually dramatizing that clothes do *not* make a lady), she takes up her absurd ostrich feather hat and assumes a fashionable air (60–61).

Shaw builds on this gaffe when she sticks out her tongue at her father, then soon declares that she would like to take a taxi to her old neighborhood and tell it to wait for her, "to put the girls in their place a bit." Notably, she says that she would not speak to them. To her, this haughty act would signal her superiority. Actually, it would conceal the fact that her speech still makes her as common as they. While Eliza's mean sentiment may pass by the audience as the humorous posturing of a downtrodden guttersnipe finally finding social muscles, Shaw plants it as the seed of a negative side to her prospects. Here, Eliza has moved from her "*innocent vanity*" at the start of the act into snobbery, a shift so striking that it even prompts Higgins to adopt a rare role for him—a socially admonishing one. To Pickering's advice that she had "better wait til we get you something really fashionable," he adds: "Besides, you shouldnt cut your old friends now that you have risen in the world. Thats what we call snobbery." This admonition offers Eliza a social concept and a new word to express it, but her gutter motives deafen her to both: "You dont call the like of them my friends now, I should hope" (62–63).

Attending to Pickering's words more than to Higgins's wiser ones, Eliza lights up at the prospect of fashionable clothes, only to reveal her lower-class origins by observing that a promised nightdress "do seem a waste of money when you could get something to shew." When Mrs. Pearce tells her that her new clothes have come, the snob howls and rushes out, climactically exposing the lady manqué and leaving Higgins and Pickering bracing themselves for the stiff job she will be.

Part of the dramatic craft of this last episode lies in its deft recapitulation of Eliza's role early in the act. Not only is she memorably framed by the doorway as she was at her first appearance, but her donning of the ostentatiously vulgar hat, her vanity, her impulse to show off in a taxi, and her howl echo the tricked-out, alternately pretentious and insecure guttersnipe of the early action. The difference now is that she has been purged of her dirty body and shabby clothes, and between Higgins's bewildering behavior, Mrs. Pearce's severity, and Pickering's kindness, a few of her simplistic notions of gentility have been shaken.

*   *   *

As the act's conclusion in the stage version of the play, the foregoing recapitulation serves much like a summary or a musical reprise before new motifs begin. A curtain at this point punctuates matters theatrically. Yet Shaw's brief extension of the action for the film works strategically, because it provides a glimpse of the purging of Eliza's gutter speech, a process that takes months. Moreover, the characterizations and pace of the added dialogue are consistent with the lively spirit of the preceding action, dramatizing tedious labors in a manner that is anything but tedious or laborious.

Shaw's description of Eliza, "feeling like a hospital out-patient at a first encounter with doctors, [one who,] but for the reassuring presence and quietude of her friend the Colonel . . . would run for her life" from the restless Higgins, befits the scene. Shaw has Higgins roaring like *"a wounded lion"* at her cockney pronunciation, despairing over "this unfortunate animal" (not noticing that he has just roared like one himself). Delighted at her aptitude one moment, then fearing she will falter the next, he threatens that "you shall be dragged round the room three times by the hair of your head" (63–64). When she weeps, he commands Pickering to give her a chocolate (as though she were an animal in training). From events earlier in the act, one might well imagine Higgins's impatience and tactlessness, counterpointed by Pickering's consolations and encouragement, during this purgatorial time, but Shaw's bright sparks here give life to such imaginings and complement the scenes that follow.

6

Act 3: Illumination

Keen observers may notice that Shaw gives dramatic energy and variety to his drama not only through contrasting characters, opinions, voices, and clothing in his scenes, but also through contrasting settings from one act to the next. Higgins's drawing room in act 2 contrasts with the street scene hubbub of act 1, and his mother's drawing room in act 3 contrasts with his quarters, which presumably look across Wimpole Street upon similar row houses. Since Shaw's description of Higgins's room mentions no windows, they must be in the "fourth wall"—toward the audience—a perspective that gives the setting a slightly claustrophobic effect. For the professor, windows or views seem of little account, except for daylight. In comparison, Mrs. Higgins enjoys a flat on the Chelsea Embankment, an extremely fashionable site, and her room has three large windows looking over the river to a park on the other side (which Shaw mentions later). The windows are open, signifying balmy weather, and serve as doors to a balcony where flowers in pots add intimate color to the sweeping view.

Shaw pointedly observes that Mrs. Higgins's room, *"which is very unlike her son's room in Wimpole Street, is not crowded with furniture and little tables and nicknacks,"* as one might expect of a late-

Cartoons of the first English cast, from *The Bystander*, 1914.
Dan H. Laurence Collection, University of Guelph Library.

Act 3: Illumination

Victorian lady in her sixties. Rather, her tastes favor airiness and elegance. While colorless classical etchings and, perhaps, prison fantasies hang on Higgins's walls, her walls feature a few good oil paintings of the romantically medieval pre-Raphaelite school and a very large landscape, and her wallpapers, window curtains, and ottoman reflect the handsome designs of William Morris, the poet and great artisan of the pre-Raphaelite school. In further strokes that link the lady to her room, Shaw specifies "*a portrait of Mrs Higgins as she was when she defied the fashion in her youth in one of the beautiful Rossettian* [pre-Raphaelite] *costumes*," but he points out that now she is "*long past taking the trouble to dress out of fashion*" (66–67).[1]

At the start of act 3, a tableau complements these distinctions: Mrs. Higgins "*sits writing at an elegantly simple writing-table*" where the only suggestion of noise is a bell button to summon servants—a contrast to her son's sound-oriented activities and clutter. The contrasts suddenly burst into action when this elegant lady is interrupted by Higgins's violent entrance through the door, "*with his hat on.*" One might say that his profession is also on. He brings Wimpole Street with him. How could such a lady have bred such a boor? There is no telling what a passion for science will do to a boy.

What is a professor to his mother? For all his eminence, he is a child in knee breeches, grown up. Mrs. Higgins removes the hat he should have taken off, tells him to go home because he offends all her friends, and calls him a good boy when he obeys her request to stop fidgeting. This is her "at-home day"—a fashionable lady's open house, a genteel time for tea and talking—hardly Henry's cup of tea. When he says he has no "small talk" (a theme soon to soar), she asks about his large talk, and when he explains that he has picked up a girl, she suspects that a girl has picked him up and exclaims "What a pity!" when she hears that this is not the case. Upon her comment that "you never fall in love with anyone under forty-five," more about his bachelorhood comes to the fore: "Oh, I cant be bothered with young women. My idea of a lovable woman is somebody as like you as possible. I shall never get into the way of seriously liking young women: some habits lie too deep to be changed. . . . Besides, theyre all idiots" (67–68).

Shaw scarcely needs Freud to suggest evidence of an Oedipus complex in this. The culture, wit, warmth, grace, understanding, and maternal authority of Mrs. Higgins would be hard for any woman to equal, let alone a young one. Intellectually acute but emotionally immature, Higgins needs mothering, even taking it from Mrs. Pearce, and his passion for science so consumes him that he seems to have little left for conventional romancing. Young women are likely to remain idiots to him because he lacks the patience to flatter or woo them. Besides, a young lady who is about to appear will affirm his generalization, degree by pathetic degree.

After Higgins tells his mother about his experiment with Eliza and informs her that he has invited the girl to her at-home, he admits to a problem that signals the limits of phonetics even to him. Although Eliza will be safe because she will "keep to two subjects: the weather and everybody's health" (his view of social small talk), a difficulty remains. He starts to explain—"You see, Ive got her pronunciation all right; but you have to consider not only *how* a girl pronounces, but what she pronounces; and thats where"—only to be cut off by the arrival of guests. The interruption turns a theatrical trick. Since Higgins is delivering strategic information, the audience is tantalized, drawn ever so slightly to the edge of its seats, then left hanging. Its response might well match Higgins's: "Oh Lord!" (69–70).

A bit like the ghost of Hamlet's father, the Eynsford Hills appear from act 1, the mother and her daughter, Clara, first, with Freddy, always tardy it seems, trailing shortly afterward. Shaw's description of the ladies sheds light on their behavior in Covent Garden and explains an edginess in them now that will add to many dramatic tensions in this act: *"The mother is well bred, quiet, and has the habitual anxiety of straitened means. The daughter has acquired a gay air of being very much at home in society: the bravado of genteel poverty."* Such anxiety and bravado, we may recall, were not strangers to Shaw, who had experienced them torturously in his youth.

The comedy that follows gains electrifying energy in the suspense with which characters teeter on, slip from, shake, or try to maintain a high wire of social decorum, starting with incongruities between social decorum and the testy indecorum of Higgins. In contrast to their contentiousness in act 1, the Eynsford Hills are on their very best behavior. This occasion, after all, is a social test of their acceptability, of their very place in such elegantly genteel quarters. The test anticipates and will soon intersect and encompass Eliza's, so that the scene becomes charged with cross-circulating tests. Higgins's peevishness punctuates and punctures the Eynsford Hills' social pleasantries, while his mother tries to control matters by frankly observing his lack of manners. When Pickering arrives for Eliza's performance, Higgins exclaims, "*over his shoulder*," "We were interrupted: damn it!" whereupon Mrs. Higgins serves decorum and her son with one suave stroke by assuring the ladies, "You couldnt have come more fortunately: we want you to meet a friend of ours." Higgins catches her meaning—"Yes, by George! We want two or three people. Youll do as well as anybody else"—only to be put out of sorts by Freddy's arrival. Freddy, with his three "Ah-de-dos" at introductions, resembles a society cretin in Oscar Wilde's *Lady Windermere's Fan* (1892) befittingly named Dumby. Such a thought could be near Higgins's lips when he asks, "What the devil are we going to talk about until Eliza comes?" and Clara Eynsford Hill, eyeing him as "*quite eligible matrimonially*," responds eagerly: "I sympathize. *I* havnt any small talk. If people would only be frank and say what they really think!" (70–73).

Given this opening for large talk, Higgins accosts the guests: "Lord forbid! . . . What they think they ought to think is bad enough, Lord knows; but what they really think would break up the whole show"; whereupon he apparently forgets himself and says what he thinks: "You see, we're all savages, more or less. We're supposed to be civilized and cultured—to know all about poetry and philosophy and art and science, and so on; but how many of us know even the meanings of these names? [*To Miss Hill*] What do *you* know of poetry? [*To Mrs. Hill*] What do *you* know of science? [*Indicating Freddy*] What does *he* know of art or science or anything else?" The truth of this might be the subject of a lively discussion, if the Hills were up to it, which they obviously are not. In a few words, it shakes not just their show but humankind's. However it scores intellectually, now it bodes social chaos.

Small talk, as Higgins has observed to his mother, is compara-tively safe, and the moment is saved only by the arrival of Eliza, well primed for it. Sheer appearance and studied grace carry off the first part of her test: "*Eliza, who is exquisitely dressed, produces an impres-sion of such remarkable distinction and beauty as she enters that they all rise, quite fluttered.*" So far, she might indeed be a duchess, or more. Guided by signals from Higgins, she introduces herself to his mother, "*speaking with pedantic correctness of pronunciation and great beauty of tone,*" a quality suggesting how carefully Higgins has deployed his tuning fork and piano. With her "How do you do, Mrs Higgins?" and her slight gasp "*in making sure of the H in Higgins,*" Shaw evokes the tension of her test, prompting the audience to share in it like parents rooting for a child in a play. He follows this tension with three "how-do-you-dos" when she is introduced to each of the Eynsford Hills—successive tests of her *h*s that sustain the tension and humor as she manages each. Only sharp listeners may notice how Shaw emphasizes Eliza's verbal distinctiveness by contrasting it with Freddy's "Ah-de-dos" barely two minutes before, illustrating the ver-bal sloppiness of some gentlemen, but no one will miss a contrast with Eliza's grace that immediately follows. After Mrs. Eynsford Hill vague-ly recalls having "met" Eliza before, Higgins suddenly remembers the family from act 1. Exclaiming, "What a damned thing!" he almost sits on his mother's elegant writing table, sulks when she objects, then stumbles noisily over the fireplace fender and fire irons before flinging himself on the divan, almost breaking it.

The "*long and painful pause*" that follows this sensational bum-bling serves at least three comic purposes: it permits the audience's laughter to subside, allows Higgins's clumsiness and his contrast with Eliza to sink in, and then, if well timed, evokes further humor through the characters' collective embarrassment and speechlessness (73–75).

As she has done before, Mrs. Higgins bridges her son's gaffe and serves his objectives gracefully while mending the social situation. Yet this time she does even more. Her conversational "Will it rain, do you think?" is hardly as incidental as the Eynsford Hills or the audience might suppose. Given her open windows, rain seems unlikely, yet "Isn't it a pleasant day?" would clash with Henry's crash. Tactfully and tactically, she is serving Eliza's turn as well as her son's by introducing one of the two topics—weather and health—that he has told her the girl can handle. Mrs. Higgins's unfailing thoughtfulness toward Eliza as a human being here and throughout the scene is a mark of her gentility. Consider the situation. Higgins has brazenly thrust not only his unsocial self but also one of his Wimpole Street experiments, a guttersnipe posing as a lady, into a social reception in her elegant drawing room. She feels driven to upbraid his boorish behavior for his own good or to explain it out of consideration for her guests, yet she would never humiliate the girl. Her kindness and gentleness resemble Pickering's, but she has even more savoir faire than he, qualities that suggest why Higgins, for all his uncouthness, finds her incomparable.

Taking the weather cue from Mrs. Higgins, Eliza pontificates: "The shallow depression in the west of these islands is likely to move slowly in an easterly direction. There are no indications of any great change in the barometrical situation." When Freddy bursts into laughter at this weather-report diction, her response—"I bet I got it right"— exposes "it" as a memorized script. Mrs. Eynsford Hill, living up to banal social form, drifts into Eliza's other topic—health—worrying about influenza if it turns cold. Apparently, Eliza has no script for influenza. Now she is on her own. Promptly rising to the challenge, she sails by personal associations into ever deeper waters. Out tumbles her aunt, who was said to have died of influenza, an allegation she does not believe because the aunt had survived diphtheria the year before when Eliza's father ladled gin down her throat. *"Piling up"* an indictment, Eliza plunges beyond her linguistic and social depth, unwittingly indicting her own genteel pretense as her grammar, idiom, and lower-class background start pulling her down: "What call would a woman with that strength in her have to die of influenza? What become of her new straw hat that should have come to me? Somebody pinched it; and what I say is, them as pinched it done her in." Thoroughly caught up in her subject, carried along by startled responses from Mrs. Eynsford Hill, she does not drop her *h*s but colorfully continues to drop not just bones of grammar but whole dancing skeletons out of her social closet: "Them she lived with would have killed her for a hat-pin, let alone a hat. . . . Gin was mother's milk to her. . . .

It never did him [her father] no harm what I could see. . . . My mother used to give him fourpence and tell him to go out and not come back until he'd drunk himself cheerful and loving-like. Theres lots of women has to make their husbands drunk to make them fit to live with" (75–77).

Early in Eliza's drift, Higgins grasps at a straw to keep the ship afloat, hastily telling Mrs. Eynsford Hill that Eliza's idiom is "the new small talk," an explanation that happily gulls and beguiles Freddy. But when Eliza ominously threatens to expose herself more expansively yet ("What I always say is—"), Higgins cuts her off: it is high time to sail away before crashing on the rocks. As goodbyes are said—calculated to trick the audience into a slight sigh of relief that all seems safe at last— Shaw triggers the climax of this most comic scene of the play by having Freddy offer to walk the young lady across the park. Eliza's response, "*with perfectly elegant diction*," catches everyone off guard: "Walk! Not bloody likely. [*Sensation*]. I am going in a taxi."

The laugh this retort evoked at the play's London premiere, the longest laugh recorded in theatrical history, came not just from the shock! and scandal! hyped by the press and eagerly anticipated by the audience, but also from its incongruity with the social scene of the play, the social pretentiousness of His Majesty's Theatre, the social milieu of the audience, and Shaw's dramatic development of its credibility. Here, Higgins's large talk and Eliza's native small talk merge. Alan Jay Lerner tried to manage an echo of its impact in *My Fair Lady* by transferring the scene to the Ascot races, where Eliza, cheering a horse, rises to a crescendo: "Come on, Dover!!! Move your bloomin' arse!!!" whereupon the racing crowd moans, several women faint, and Pickering flees the scene while Higgins roars with laughter.[2] Not bad. But Lerner avoided *bloody*. It had lost its punch. Alas, modern theater may never resurrect its impact, which, as Shaw placed it, delivered a coup of topical humor. But the scene it climaxes offers a cornucopia of comedy as it is.

Aside from the jolt of *bloody*, the humor of Eliza's response springs from the ways it compacts and caps a host of comic elements. It climaxes the scene's highly articulated, wild incongruity between audacious social pretension and squalid human realities. Eliza's supernal elegance and grace are accretively punctured by her wretchedly lower-class subject matter. Her complete seriousness about bizarre details of her subject makes her delivery all the funnier. Refined diction mixes with grammatical incompetence. Extremes of high humor mix with low humor, naive humor with black humor, irony with farce, all of which are energized by the tensions of her social test and her fraudulence and played off against a family whose pretenses are also being tested. Mrs. Eynsford Hill's startled, appalled responses counterpoint Eliza's unconscious self-revelation, adding zest for the play's audience, which finds itself both observing and experiencing Eliza's test and performance while she is slipping, then propped by Higgins, then slipping, slipping (will she? won't she? will she?), only barely pulling matters off, until finally, within a hair's-breadth of success, she drops a bombshell—completely unaware that she has done so.

A further aspect of this comic abundance rises from qualities of Eliza shown here that correspond to comic qualities we have observed in Higgins as he combines a machinelike professional temperament with a humanly diverse personality. The elegant, graceful young lady at the start of the scene who impresses the group and tickles Freddy with her robotically memorized, precisely articulated weather report has many elements of an ingeniously contrived machine. In this sense, she resembles Olympia in Offenbach's *Tales of Hoffman*, a beautiful, life-sized mechanical doll that enraptures Hoffman much as Eliza enraptures Freddy. Higgins, it would seem, has created a mechanical triumph. Yet what makes the situation both touching and comic are hints that inside this doll breathes a human being struggling with her diction, especially her *h*s. The doll operates superbly—grotesquely so—when Mrs. Higgins triggers her weather-report switch. But when Mrs. Eynsford Hill switches the subject to influenza, a topic for which the doll is not programmed, its wiring short-circuits, allowing the nascent human being within it to come out. It continues to operate according to much of its circuited diction, but the circuits lose control of what it is saying, giving the impression of a machine out of control. As with Frankenstein's monster, the effect could be horrifying. To Higgins, it almost proves so; to Mrs. Eynsford Hill, it literally is. The danger, however, is the opposite of monstrous: it lies only in the emerging human being. In short, the short-circuiting is life-oriented, creative, expansive, funny, and joyous.

Much as Doolittle is a natural rhetorician, the Eliza who emerges proves herself a natural storyteller. While rich irony lies in her being most funny when she is most serious, even richer irony lies in the colorful farce of the squalid life she reveals, a farce through which Shaw sharply images its opposite: the sordidness Eliza seeks to grow beyond—illness, deprivation, murder, thievery, alcoholism. Having briefly but memorably illlustrated his point about poverty's relation to debasement and crime, Shaw has Eliza's narrative evolve beyond ratiocination about her aunt's death to the love of her mother for her father, with the prospect of a personal commentary evolving from this when Higgins, sensing that the *real* Eliza will send his doll wildly out of control and utterly destroy its social credibility, presses a stop button.

Finally, "I'm going in a taxi" climaxes Shaw's taxi theme. The perfectly elegant diction Eliza lends to this utterance transcends her faltering grammar and resurrects the doll, whose machinery befits a taxi. Yet the declaration brings her life to the fore. Walking is as demeaning for her as it was for Clara in act 1. It is the necessary mode of the deprived class that she intends to leave behind and that Clara never wants to resemble. No matter how black or sputtering London taxis may be, they are the carriages of a privileged existence. Therefore, as in act 1, if Freddy wants to walk, he must walk alone.

Less sensational but just as symbolic as the taxi theme is the problem of the Eynsford Hills, which Shaw also introduces at the start of the play and develops in this act and the next. Mrs. Eynsford Hill speaks first after Eliza leaves: "Well, I really cant get used to the new ways"; whereupon Clara, discontented, declares: "Oh, it's all right, mamma, quite right. People will think we never go anywhere or see anybody if you are so old-fashioned." While Mrs. Eynsford Hill dislikes Clara "talking about men as rotters and calling everything filthy and beastly" (sentiments suggesting that Clara may never be far from filth and beastliness herself), the young lady, determined to be up on the latest fashion, finds Eliza's new small talk delightful. As they leave, she mentions that they are going to three more at-homes (the sheer number signaling a desperate desire to climb socially). Higgins, playing the devil as he does with Eliza in act 2, urges her to try the new small talk at them. When she smilingly agrees, calling Victorian prudery nonsense, he, "*tempting her*," calls it "such damned nonsense!" Falling for this demonic bait, she exclaims, "Such bloody nonsense!" and goes out radiantly, "*conscious of being thoroughly up to date*," blissfully unaware that she is about to dig her social grave (78–79).

Mrs. Eynsford Hill, her eyes moist, provides a moment of pathos by speaking privately to Mrs. Higgins before she joins her daughter. Her plight offers an upper-class version of Eliza's recent account of poverty: "You mustnt mind Clara. . . . We're so poor! and she gets so few parties, poor child! She doesnt quite know. . . . But the boy is nice. Dont you think so?" (80). Mrs. Higgins, of course, is compassionate, and for anyone in the audience who has missed the Eynsford Hills' problem, this presents it clearly. It would appear that Eliza has passed her test not only through her talents and Higgins's efforts to save her, but also because the Eynsford Hills are not especially bright and are all too eager to be accepted into genteel society themselves.

Being a young lady yet poor, Clara is psychologically on edge because she finds herself at the edge of respectability, sensitive about her prerogatives because she can boast so few, eagerly seeking a place she cannot afford. Thus, she is a disagreeable bundle of vanity, defense mechanisms, and false hopes. Her calling men "rotters" echoes her calling Freddy a "pig" in act 1 (15). Her violent response to Higgins as a stranger then—"Will you please keep your impertinent remarks to yourself" (25)—contrasts with her playing up to him as the son of Mrs. Higgins now. Her scorn for the flower girl then contrasts with her reverent attitude sitting alongside the fashionable Eliza now, "*devouring her with her eyes*" (75). In many ways, she resembles the flower girl who vainly donned the ostrich feather hat to complement a simple kimono in act 2, eliciting Higgins's comment, "A new fashion, by George!" (61). Such warps in her character may be pitied more than censured. Socially living for one at-home after another, residing in quarters too humble to have elegant at-homes herself, too poor to afford clothes like Eliza's, and neither as attractive nor as charming as she, with few prospects matrimonial or otherwise, longing for glamour, longing to *belong*, Clara seems consigned forever to the fringe of upper-class social life, a frustrating prospect that renders her too eager, too aggressive, too abrasive, too pretentious, too parasitic, and too cynically confused to be acceptable in the genteel class to which she presumably belongs.

One should notice how smoothly Shaw modulates the play's mood from the hilarity of Eliza's test to the lesser comedy of Clara's adoption of her "small talk," to this somber note that brings the action back to serious concerns about Eliza. Simultaneously, he moves the Eynsford Hills offstage, characterizes them poignantly, provides the audience with a psychological transition, and emphasizes a thematic point that he soon applies to Eliza.

Shifting from the pathos of the Eynsford Hills, the end of the act's stage version develops a new tension between two perspectives on Eliza: the troubled concerns of Mrs. Higgins, and the ebullient views of Higgins and Pickering. Higgins receives a dose of reality therapy when he eagerly asks his mother if Eliza is presentable: "You silly boy, of course she's not presentable. She's a triumph of your art and of her dressmaker's; but if you suppose for a moment that she doesnt give herself away in every sentence she utters, you must be perfectly cracked about her." Notably, she refers to her son's profession as his "art," not science, and introduces the possibility that his deafness to Eliza's social gaffes involves some sort of affection. Otherwise, Mrs. Higgins advances a version of Mrs. Pearce's concerns about what is to become of Eliza, yet hers emerge more clearly because Eliza is not present to distract attention, and more forcefully because of her genteel sophistication. Might they eliminate the sanguinary element from Eliza's conversation? asks Pickering. "Not as long as she is in Henry's hands." On what terms is Eliza staying at Wimpole Street? she asks. Each man mentions a "silly bee" in Mrs. Pearce's bonnet (thus giving the bee more sting): "She keeps saying 'You dont think, sir'" (80–81).

Vehemently contradicting this admonition, Higgins delivers a remarkable view of what he has done: "I'm worn out, thinking about her, and watching her lips and her teeth and her tongue, not to mention her soul, which is the quaintest of the lot."

Soul? . . .

Act 3: Illumination

Ignoring the word, Mrs. Higgins responds aptly to the rest: "You certainly are a pretty pair of babies, playing with your live doll." Irate, Higgins exclaims: "Playing! The hardest job I ever tackled. . . . But you have no idea how frightfully interesting it is to take a human being and change her into quite a different human being by creating a new speech for her. It's filling up the deepest gulf that separates class from class and soul from soul" (81–82). "Frightfully" may well describe the interest of taking and changing a human being into quite a different human being. "Creating" suggests an aspect of Pygmalion's art in his science of speech. Eliza's test has offered partial evidence of phonetics "filling up the deepest gulf that separates class from class." But what about filling the gulf that separates "soul from soul"?

In discerning that the hardest job of his life involves matters of soul, and in finding himself at the "frightfully interesting" center of transmuting a human being from one state to a higher one through his creative powers, Higgins voices a spiritual thrill and conviction, not just high-flying hyperbole. We may recall hyperbole throughout the play about social matters and change, but even when it is comic it has spiritual undertones or overtones. The blinding lightning and rattling thunder that coincide with the collision of Eliza and Freddy at the start of act 1 deliver the bang of hyperbole in action—a divinely inspired, satiric joke; nonetheless, it occurs. Following his phonetics performance later in that act, Higgins's order that Eliza stop her boohooing, "or else seek a shelter of some other place of worship," may elicit a smile, until he tops it by declaring that "a woman who utters such depressing and disgusting sounds has no right to be anywhere—no right to live. Remember that you are a human being with a soul and the divine gift of articulate speech" (27). When, shortly after asserting that he could pass her off as a duchess or the Queen of Sheba, he throws her money in answer to *"the voice of God"* in a church clock, the gesture has a light touch of whimsy, yet his charity means salvation for her (28). By capriciously playing the tempter in act 2, declaring that if Eliza refuses the experiment the angels will weep for her, he is at least partly on the angels' side. Despite the positive results of these occasions, however, their fancy, hyperbole, and fun seem stronger than their conviction.

Now when Higgins earnestly repeats the terms "human being" and "soul" from act 1, the conviction has more power. Higgins's vigorous expression of the spiritual import of what he has done is important not just in itself but also for its retrospective effect: it casts a light on key portions of his preceding fancy and hyperbole as well as on the idea of change so frequently forwarded in the play, reilluminating them as omens of a spiritual change.

Such emphases came naturally to Shaw. Religious themes, often unconventionally expressed and linked to social matters, are at the heart of many of his plays. A month before he started *Pygmalion*, he had written *Androcles and the Lion*, in which he turned the classic legend (about a Christian saved by a lion he had once helped) into a fable about the diverse nature of faith. As Higgins links phonetics and social change, he presents a modern version of such spiritual diversity while also echoing a classic legend.

Social and religious themes join here in the nature of Higgins's ambitions and the phases of Eliza's growth. Higgins's exaltation of articulate speech as a "divine gift" in act 1 is no exaggeration for him. The profession that fills his soul involves a faith in the distinctively human and divine powers of articulation, a faith that melds "Shakespear and Milton and The Bible" (27) as ultimate examples of articulation, a faith reflecting the gospel according to St. John, where Genesis starts with "In the beginning was the Word, and the Word was with God, and the Word was God." As Christ, according to John, became the human articulation of the Word, human beings, for Higgins, may realize their distinctive spirituality through articulating their souls.

The howl with which Eliza responds to Higgins's disparagement of her sounds dramatizes his point. In one sense, she is a "disgrace to the noble [Greek] architecture of these [church] columns": her debasement contrasts with the classical and Christian origins of St. Paul's portico. A potential streetwalker, she would be grist for a Pauline epistle. Her class is not far from the first prostitutes who made a misogynist of the mythical Pygmalion. In another sense, she is also, as Higgins calls her, a "creature": she follows her first howl with three more in act 1 and eight in act 2. The howls represent quite different feelings or thoughts: wonder, terror, rebelliousness, bewilderment, objection, protest, deprecation, humiliation, dazzlement, excitement. Yet such distinctions are blurred in the generalized impresssion of overflowing emotion from an underprivileged waif—or animal.

Shaw images this last resemblance in act 2 when Eliza turns *"at bay,"* then howls, *"wounded and whimpering."* He suggests a specific animal when Higgins orders Mrs. Pearce to scrub her with "Monkey Brand" if necessary, and again when Doolittle declares, "I cant carry the girl through the streets like a blooming monkey, can I?" (41, 57). Later, in Eliza's training scene for the film, Higgins refers to her as "this unfortunate animal" (64). One may guess what an animal's howl expresses less by its sound than by its context. Similarly, Eliza's howls lack the discriminations that distinguish humans—an articulate expression of what she means.

By perceiving Eliza's plight as that of one who lacks the means to realize her human potential and soul, Higgins assumes a temporal and spiritual role similar to that of King Solomon, whose wisdom, wealth, and spirituality so impressed the Queen of Sheba. Yet act 3 signals his illumination as well as Eliza's. Hardly a Solomon, the professor has discovered that phonetics answers only to part of her problem. His comment to his mother that "you have to consider not only *how* a girl pronounces, but what she pronounces" (70) is amply confirmed when Eliza slips into her colorful rendition of her squalid background and is doubly confirmed when Mrs. Higgins observes that the girl gives herself away with every sentence she utters. To win his bet, and perhaps to realize her soul fully, Eliza will need more than this Pygmalion has given her.

Meanwhile, to perceive Eliza's evolution clearly, one must counter Higgins's view of it with a perspective much closer to hers. Professionally, she reveals adroit street smarts in act 1. With her native intelligence and experience telling her where she stands and how one copes as a flower girl, she makes the most of her limited options. Spiritually, she clutches at a distinction extremely important to her: she finds self-respect in being virtuous, "a good girl," sexually and perhaps otherwise. Initially, Higgins notices only her slum dialect and the fact that she is a nuisance to him, while she is panicked by the possibility that he may be a police informer, then hurt by his lack of consideration, complaining, tellingly, "He's no right to take away my character. My character is the same as any lady's" (26). But when he repeats her howl, tickling her native humor, her attention is drawn to his boast that he could pass her off as a duchess or get her a place as a lady's maid or shop assistant.

The personal possibilities in this come to her like a spark in the night (her version of a flash of lightning), but she has no funds to realize her awakening. Earlier, God was in lightning. Now he's in St. Paul's clock, providentially playing into her hands via the professor's hands when he throws her enough change to enable her change. Suddenly, this downtrodden Cinderella, always a good girl beneath her smudges and ragged clothes, can indulge her exuberance in a fanciful carriage to "Bucknam Pellis." What are her dreams when she sleeps that night? We soon discover that they probably combined Cinderella's with reality. Inverting the order of the change Higgins said he could give her, she chooses "shop assistant" but alters this to "a *lady* in a flower shop," not realizing that the only real ladies in flower shops are customers. According to her intelligence, virtue, and good sense, and on the principle that God helps those who help themselves, she capitalizes on her good fortune the next morning by capitalizing on her capacities, extending her Cinderella carriage ride to a practical palace on Wimpole Street.

Although in her eyes an ostrich feather hat transforms her into a latter-day Cinderella, or, more specifically, into a "lady," Eliza's Cinderella dreams and sense of gentility go through purgatory in Higgins's weird establishment. She could hardly hope for Prince Charming, but she does not expect a monster, especially when she is willing to pay a huge sum (to her) for lessons. Like many monsters, this one changes aspects. At moments, he storms or bullies or mystifies, at others, he cajoles or apparently tries to seduce her. Variously terrified, bewildered, and suspicious, of one thing she is sure: he is no gentleman. Ultimately, he is a devil; more immediately, he is a sly rake who tempts her with chocolates and taxis and gold and diamonds. He instructs his accomplice, his severe housekeeper, to strip her, burn her clothes, and wallop her (like a cruel stepmother) if she objects. Were it not for intercession by a kindly old gentleman and her own deep desire for gentility, she would flee. The purgation of a bath and clearer prospects of gentility, however, suggest that she can remain a good girl and become a lady too. And after the punishing purgation of her speech through lessons, then her test in act 3, that, apparently, is what she has indeed become. She has a moment to bask in her Cinderella transformation and her illumination as a lady, both worlds beyond the Covent Garden flower girl who struggled, against all odds, for survival and her virtue.

Still, what about her soul, which Higgins now describes, even above his phonetic labors with her, as "the quaintest of the lot"? Contrary to the professor, one may agree with some critics that the Eliza of act 3 is less alive and more doll-like than the Eliza of acts 1 and 2. Yet the situation is more ambiguous than that. In certain respects, the Eliza of act 3 is a sensational version of Clara. Like Clara, she is on her best behavior, acting up to a social test. More significant than her ladylike veneer, however, is the graphic way the flower girl inside her breaks vitally through the veneer, providing glimpses of her social background. This recalls the Eliza of act 1, the girl who energetically and cannily pursued her trade, showed a sense of the proper role of a mother in her response to Freddy's mother, clung to her dignity and honor, abided by the law as best she could, spontaneously laughed when Higgins mimicked her howl, and wisely decided to seek him out for lessons—all signs that Higgins has been working with more inborn aspects of soul than he seems to realize.

An Achilles heel of Eliza's soul is her vanity. In act 1, her pride in being a good girl amounts to a personal virtue beyond a mere sense of propriety. It gives her a core of integrity and spirit when she has little else to hang on to. Her pride tips toward vanity, however, when she indulges in fantasy and wish fulfillment by taking the taxi. Then, when she leaves the taxi, uttering "impidence" at the taxi driver's familiarity, a snobbery resembling Clara's briefly surfaces. Her reaction may be pardoned since she is humiliated by the taxi driver undercutting her show, yet it presents the first instance of a negative development. Pride in one's virtue and honor is one thing, but asserting one's superiority over others is vanity, a pride of a different ilk. In act 2, Higgins's money and her lucky fortune again move Eliza's pride toward vanity, then snobbery. Early in the act, she responds to Mrs. Pearce, "Oh we *are* proud!" (38), and though this slight is thwarted by Higgins's assaults, vanity and snobbery reemerge when she dons her feather hat, then desires to take a taxi and snub her old friends. Under the pressures of her test in act 3, these qualities are subverted again, only to leap forth in her *bloody* response to Freddy. Although her haughtiness is undercut by her origins, it increasingly echoes Clara's. Thus, Shaw uses his taxi theme for yet another purpose, showing how far Eliza has to go before her gentility can resemble the real article, as embodied in Mrs. Higgins.

Higgins's interest in Eliza's soul springs largely from his presumption that he is creating it, but when he and Pickering assail his mother's ears about their work with Eliza, one may sense paradoxically that Eliza, in a way, is creating them. In any case, the debt is two-sided. Most revealing is Higgins's comment that "she regularly fills our lives up," a point rapidly illustrated as they alternately explain how they are always talking Eliza, teaching, dressing, and inventing new Elizas. Enthusiastically speaking at the same time, Higgins extols her quick ear and precocity with dialects while Pickering extols her genius in music and playing the piano. Readers may be thankful that in print one can follow the speakers separately, because nowhere else are Eliza's impressive aptitudes so clearly set forth. Audiences are less lucky. Directors and actors might well orchestrate the men's simultaneity so that key clauses and phrases stand out, such as Higgins's "She has the most extraordinary quickness of ear . . . every possible sort of sound . . . Continental dialects, African dialects . . . she picks them up like a shot . . . as if she had been at it all her life," and Pickering's "that girl is a genius. She can play the piano . . . classical concerts and to music halls . . . she plays everything she hears right off . . . Brahms or Lehar . . . months ago, she'd never as much as touched a piano" (82–83).

This rapid-fire duet climaxes the men's obsession with their experiment by articulating their absorption in the processes of "creating" Eliza and their amazed, new appreciation of her as a person with remarkable capacities. This appreciation, notably, reveals that their experiment and creative processes are only partly responsible for her success. Their financing and work have enabled her native talents—talents that had little opportunity, incentive, or encouragement to develop in her life of poverty—now to blossom. The men have been facilitators of her genius. She is serving both their creation and realizing her own. At heart, the creative process has been a collaboration.

Shushing them, Mrs. Higgins brings the men back to her concern: a Problem. Pickering assumes that this lies in how to pass Eliza off as a lady. Higgins's comment, "I'll solve that problem. Ive half solved it already," not only resurrects his awareness early in the act that phonetics will be only half the story but asserts, against ample evidence of his social bumbling, that he can take care of a half that lies outside his profession. Both overlook the fact that Eliza herself has surmounted what could have been their greatest difficulty: the aptitude of the student to absorb a professor's lessons. So there have been three problems: Eliza's speech, the need to hurdle her impoverished background, and the question of her ability to learn.

But in addition to these, Mrs. Higgins is introducing a more troubling personal issue. (Why is it that men cannot see what is obvious to a woman?) Dressing the men down, she reiterates Mrs. Pearce's concern: "No, you two infinitely stupid male creatures: the problem of what is to be done with her afterwards." Her calling them "creatures" manages what Mrs. Pearce did not dare. To Higgins, Eliza has been the creature. Now he, a creature, misses his mother's point: "I dont see anything in that. She can go her own way, with all the advantages I have given her." Whereupon Mrs. Higgins takes a great step beyond Mrs. Pearce, to Mrs. Eynsford Hill: "The advantages of that poor woman who was here just now! The manners and habits that disqualify a fine lady from earning her own living without giving her a fine lady's income! Is that what you mean?" The stupid males breeze past her concern—"We'll find her some light employment"—"There are plenty of openings. We'll do whats right. Goodbye"—and go off, relishing the thought of Eliza mimicking people after a Shakespeare exhibition (a reference that echoes their recent praise of her talents and, ironically, Higgins's citation of Shakespeare in act 1 as an example of the language Eliza defiled). Left to herself, Mrs. Higgins ends the stage version of the act frustrated with the age-old burden of women: "Oh, men! men!! men!!!" (84).

Mrs. Higgins's reference to Mrs. Eynsford Hill to highlight a problem in store for Eliza illustrates Shaw's fertile use of minor characters to develop major themes. Clara has provided telling parallels with Eliza; now her mother foreshadows trouble in Eliza's future, and Freddy will soon evolve as another foil. Mrs. Higgins's stark irony in lifting her son's phrase about "all the advantages" he has given Eliza, then her attack on his presumption with the example of Mrs. Eynsford Hill, should forcefully drive home her point for him (and for the audience). She is cutting right to the core of the problem with scientific pursuits that are thoughtless or careless about human results. Her term "poor" for Mrs. Eynsford Hill carries a double impact: Mrs. Eynsford Hill is poor both because she has few funds and because poverty makes her particularly pitiful. The pathos lies not so much in poverty itself as in the deflation, humiliation, and sham that poverty can wreak on a woman bred as a "fine" lady. While Clara is scarcely a fine lady, Shaw suggests that Mrs. Eynsford Hill, but for her pathetic, apologetic, money-scrimping circumstances, may deserve the term nearly as much as Mrs. Higgins. She was born in a country mansion. She is gentle, patient, kindly. Understanding how her children's problems relate to poverty, she makes painful allowances for Clara's insecurity and abrasiveness. Mrs. Higgins can be frank with Henry because he is not vulnerable and neither is she. Mrs. Eynsford Hill cannot be frank with her children because they are very vulnerable and so is she.

Higgins fails to appreciate how his original boast that he could make Eliza into a duchess or a shop assistant has led to the problem of the great disparity between the two. Eliza naively bridges the disparity at first by wanting to be a lady in a flower shop. To most effects and purposes, she qualifies for that goal by now. Higgins's bet with Pickering and his fascination with his experiment, however, are aimed at making her a duchess, and this goal, plus the almost duchesslike clothes he dresses her in, have shifted Eliza toward an utterly make-believe social status. Far beyond playing a lady in a flower shop, she must have attributes of a fine lady to play a fine lady well. Then what? Higgins's answer lies in "light employment," Pickering's in "plenty of openings." The answers suggest a shop assistant. For one trained to be a truly "fine" lady? This is Mrs. Higgins's concern, a problem the men, and Eliza, fail to foresee.

*   *   *

The absence of the ambassador's reception scene in the stage version of the play may seem lamentable to those familiar with *Pygmalion*'s film version or *My Fair Lady*. In preparing for the play's production at Canada's annual Niagara-on-the-Lake Shaw Festival in 1992, the festival's artistic director decided to include the scene and even had costumes prepared for it, but then shelved the notion: "Would anyone care to buy some elegant costumes, cheap?" His foray and retreat may be pardoned, with sympathy. Aside from the difficulty and cost of staging the scene's cinematic elements, a good reason not to include it is that Shaw felt it superfluous. Act 3 had already given him the chance to show Eliza developing, providing rich humor in her slips between a genteel occasion and her squalid origins. Her very success at the ambassador's reception, in contrast, would depend on her *not* slipping. Could much real drama or character development occur in elegant pretense? At the embassy, he could display little more than Higgins's doll and a social response to it, not much about Eliza. Having more taste and dramatic discretion than Cecil B. DeMille, he lacked DeMille's instincts for sheer spectacle.

In his added film scene, however, Shaw manages to combine touches of DeMille's world and his own by creating the suspense of a new test, this time not playing Eliza against insecure, overeager, easily gulled gentlefolk, but against a presumed expert in languages and dialects, an exploitive Hungarian busybody and former student of Higgins, Nepommuck.

The scene actually revolves more around Nepommuck as a tester than around Eliza, yet his test and the social milieu do provide new insights about her. Shaw (via Pickering's funds) gives Eliza her Cinderella carriage, not a taxi this time but a Rolls-Royce (which he demeans as a "car"), an opera cloak, an evening dress, diamonds, and accessories. Moreover, when Pickering admits that he is nervous—"I feel exactly as I felt before my first battle"—Shaw reveals her early Cinderella fantasies: "It is not the first time for me, Colonel. I have done this fifty times—hundreds of times—in my little piggery in Angel Court in my day-dreams. I am in a dream now." More subtly, he also defines her distinctiveness by describing her as one who has "*a beautiful gravity that awes her hostess*," as one who combines her background, her training, and the pressure of the occasion to become "so intent on her ordeal that she walks like a somnambulist in a desert instead of a débutante in a fashionable crowd," a phenomenon that stops the crowd's talk (as occurs in "Cinderella") when they "look at her, admiring her dress, her jewels, and her strangely attractive self" (85–93).

Higgins's comment to the hostess—"How do you do? Fearful bore for you this sort of thing. Forgive my part in it"—might almost come from Shaw: how boring such occasions, in which fashion counts for so much and intelligence for so little, can be. Yet Shaw has already given zest to this one: the hostess comments that Miss Doolittle "will make a sensation" (an echo of the sensation Eliza formerly provoked with her *bloody*), then asks Nepommuck to find out all about her. When the Hungarian returns, declaring Eliza "a fraud," Shaw momentarily takes the scene's breath away. Rapidly, however, he shifts from the appalling to the amazing as Nepommuck finds her "Hungarian. And of royal blood. . . . Only the Magyar races can produce that air of the divine right, those resolute eyes. She is a princess" (93–94). Thus, Eliza answers royally not only to the upper-crust social scene, to Pickering's bet, and to Cinderella fantasies, but also, with a sense of "divine right," to Higgins's declaration in act 1 that she defiled "the divine gift of articulate speech." Eliza's somnambulent concentration on her ordeal has given her royally resolute eyes that distinguish her beauty; her unbelievable ignorance in identifying Nepommuck's Hungarian as French has convinced him not that she is as phony as he but that, like himself, she is artfully duplicitous, knowing both languages.

By having Nepommuck explain that she is "not necessarily legitimate, of course. Morganatic perhaps. But that is undoubtedly her class," Shaw satirically cinches her presumed relationship to royalty. Earlier in this scene, the hostess has heard the sensation Eliza causes compared to that evoked by Mrs. Langtry (a famous beauty who was mistress to Edward VII). In act 5, Doolittle admits that Eliza is illegitimate (124). Here, the hostess admits to being terrified at meeting her—"I had a schoolmistress who talked like that"—and Eliza reports, "An old lady has just told me that I speak exactly like Queen Victoria" (a "good girl" if there ever was one, whose native German, like Eliza's cockney, was "foreign"). So Shaw mixes her pretension, her realities, and her analogies to royalty, both scandalous and virtuous, in provocative ways.

Most telling and ambiguous personally, at last, is Eliza's comment to Higgins and Pickering as they are about to leave: "I dont think I can bear much more. . . . I am sorry if I have lost your bet. I have done my best; but nothing can make me the same as these people" (95). Pickering assures her that she has won the bet ten times over, yet she seems to have won something far more important: while her remark could reflect despair that she will never be in the same class with "these people," more likely it reflects distaste and a touch of disdain for the social "desert" they inhabit. Perhaps it includes despair, distaste, and disdain all at once: a new illumination that, beyond Cinderella fantasies, justifies the scene.

7

Act 4: The Dark Night of Eliza's Soul

The issue of Eliza's soul, which Shaw weaves through phonetics, social themes, Cinderella fantasies, Pygmalion motifs, and touches of a devil in the first three acts, emerges traumatically in act 4. Readers of the text (with its embassy scene), unlike audiences of the stage version, may tend to forget that in most theater productions the Eliza portrayed here follows the one who produced a sensation as she left Mrs. Higgins's drawing room to ride off in a taxi. Now she is a lady who has passed a test not only at the ambassador's reception but also, as Pickering tells us, at a garden party (the locale originally specified in his bet with Higgins) and a dinner party as well. And since the Eliza of act 3 was performing up to a test—or tests, if we include the reception—we have barely glimpsed her as a non-role-playing individual since she was a guttersnipe with pretensions in act 2, at least six months before.

Once again, Shaw evokes a fairy-tale association as the clock on Higgins's mantelpiece strikes twelve (*My Fair Lady* misses his point, having it strike three). Just as the ball is over at midnight for Cinderella, so it is for Eliza. In one of his rare slips, Shaw describes this as a summer night, calling up the same season suggested in act 3 by

Act 4: The Dark Night of Eliza's Soul

Mrs. Higgins's open windows and specified in the heavy summer rain of act 1. Since the professor's bet with Pickering was for three to six months (and the colonel refers to six in act 3), apparently summer has been preternaturally long this year. Perhaps it is no great matter when a fairy tale, even a "realistic" one, is set in the ambiance of eternal summer. But late fall or winter would seem appropriate for the moods to come as Eliza takes off her cloak and gloves, and Higgins and Pickering take off their hats and overcoats. At first, the men are like teenage boys who have come home late. Pickering comments, "I say: Mrs Pearce will row if we leave these things lying about in the drawing room," and Higgins responds, "Oh, chuck them over the bannisters into the hall. . . . She'll think we were drunk." Pickering's comment, "We are, slightly," helps explain nuances and extremities in the following action (96–97).

In contrast to both the tipsy, conversational men and her own chattiness in act 3, Eliza, who has put on the lights, is brooding and silent. Shaw observes that *"she is tired: her pallor contrasts strongly with her dark eyes and hair; and her expression is almost tragic."* When Higgins exclaims, "I wonder where the devil my slippers are!" she *"looks at him darkly,"* then fetches them, placing them on the carpet near him. After commenting on the "silly tomfoolery" of the evening, he sees the slippers, *"as if they had appeared there of their own accord,"* and soon exclaims, "Thank God it's over!" Neither man notices that *"Eliza flinches violently"* (96–98).

Virtually unconscious of Eliza's presence, Higgins complains about "the strain of putting the job through all these months. . . . It was interesting enough at first, while we were at the phonetics; but after that I got deadly sick of it. . . . It was a silly notion: the whole thing has been a bore . . . nobody but a damned fool of a fashionable woman to talk to! . . . No more artificial duchesses. The whole thing has been simple purgatory." Thus, he thinks of the strain as his and reduces Eliza to a job that was a silly notion, a bore, simple purgatory for him. Notably, he lost interest after the phonetic portion of her training, presumably after act 3, at the point when Eliza had to be tutored not about how to speak but about what to say, matters that could well have been most important in developing her soul. Pickering is more generous, giving fuller dimensions to her achievement: "I was quite frightened once or twice because Eliza was doing it so well. You see, lots of the real people cant do it at all: theyre such fools that they think style comes by nature to people in their position; and so they never learn." But even he forgets to address her, bidding Higgins goodnight with, "Still, it's been a great occasion: a triumph for you," after Higgins has declared, "It's over and done with; and now I can go to bed at last without dreading tomorrow." Neither has noticed how *"Eliza's beauty becomes murderous"* at Higgins's implication that, since her training is over and done with, he is free from the tedium of working with her (the boring, purgatorial job) tomorrow. Following Pickering out, he speaks *"over his shoulder"* to her for the first time in the scene, as though ordering his parlormaid: "Put out the lights, Eliza; and tell Mrs Pearce not to make coffee for me in the morning: I'll take tea" (98–99).

Were an audience to focus primarily on the speakers in this scene, it could miss the fact that Eliza's reactions are fully as important as what is being said. Shaw draws attention to her by having Higgins throw himself into the easy chair at the hearth, which is to the forestage on the left, while Eliza sits stonily on the long piano bench to the forestage at the right. Thus, the stage is divided between the two, highlighting both, while Pickering moves in between. After Higgins leaves, she commands attention as she walks across the stage to the hearth to turn off the lights. Inner turmoil tenses her like a spring, then snaps into action: *"By the time she gets there she is on the point of screaming. She sits down in Higgins's chair and holds on hard to the arms. Finally she gives way and flings herself furiously on the floor, raging"* (100). The shock of this is doubled by its appalling contrast with her elegant, bejeweled, ladylike appearance.

By having Higgins reappear at this moment, expressing *"despairing wrath"* because he cannot find his slippers, Shaw juxtaposes two rages—Eliza's deep one and Higgins's petty one—a dramatic effect that heightens emotions and contrasts them, to Higgins's disfavor. Then, within an instant, and more important, he has Eliza hurl the slippers at Higgins—"Take your slippers; and may you never have a day's luck with them!"—sensationally twisting the play's Cinderella motif, and climaxing it.

Much as Cinderella had to return to domestic realities after the clock struck twelve, so has Eliza. For Cinderella, however, the loss of a slipper led an attentive prince to discover her identity, fulfilling their romance. Higgins's behavior over his lost slippers, in contrast, confuses Eliza's identity, shows his lack of appreciation for her, and augurs no fulfillment. His utter indifference to her may even be worse than ingratitude. The flower girl who has slaved to become a lady, has served his ends in doing so, and has just been immensely admired and hailed as a princess, now humbly plays the servant to a man who fails to notice, who has tossed her a command over his shoulder and inadvertently cursed her kind attention to his comfort.

Thus, Shaw develops a detail into a memorable symbol that reflects on Higgins's and Eliza's characters and their relationship, a symbol given extra point as it contrasts with a slipper that plays a crucial role in a famous fairy tale. In hurling the slippers at this uncharming prince, Eliza violently rejects her Cinderella dreams.

The ensuing dialogue takes violent swings, both between the two characters and as it vents radical shifts in the temper of each. Higgins is in command as he pulls Eliza up from her rage on the floor: "Get up. . . . Anything wrong?" Breathless, she puts her feelings and the situation on the line: "Nothing wrong—with you. Ive won your bet for you, havnt I? Thats enough for you. *I* dont matter, I suppose." His response treats her sentiments as a bald challenge: "You won my bet! You! Presumptuous insect! *I* won it." Her declaration presents a version of her Cinderella impulses. Unlike Cinderella, however, she had to work hard for success. Higgins ignores her efforts. Like a Pygmalion, he considers himself her creator: through his art, he has turned a squashed cabbage leaf into a lady. The actual situation, we have noticed, is more complex than either view, but the play tilts more toward Eliza's perspective than his. We may recall Pickering commenting at the end of the embassy scene that Eliza had won the bet "ten times over," and Shaw observing at the start of this act that *"she has just won Higgins's bet for him."* Egotistically spinning past such considerations, Higgins asks, "What did you throw those slippers at me for?" Eliza blurts out her emotions: "Because I wanted to smash your face. I'd like to kill you, you selfish brute. Why didnt you leave me where you picked me out of—in the gutter? You thank God it's all over, and that now you can throw me back again there, do you?" Observing her frantic agitation *"in cool wonder,"* Higgins delivers a cruel blow—"The creature is nervous, after all"—whereupon she *"gives a suffocated scream of fury, and instinctively darts her nails at his face."* He catches her wrists, throwing her roughly into the easy chair: "Claws in, you cat. How dare you shew your temper to me? Sit down and be quiet" (100).

Less sensational but more deeply rooted in this passage than its violent action is its revelation of changes in Eliza that underlie her rejection of Cinderella dreams and reflect against Higgins. For her, the tensions of her test have transferred to apprehensions about her place in the world. Her social success, however great, has been momentary, a triumph of pretense and make-believe nearly as unreal as Cinderella's. The euphoria of triumphs may often be followed by a let-down in the face of life's mundane realities, and Eliza's realities are particularly unstable and discouraging. Beforehand she could aim at the test; now she finds aimlessness. She is dislocated, fit for neither high nor low society. Rather than reassuring or helping her, Pickering has congratulated Higgins, while Higgins, feeling a let-down himself, has called the whole thing a bore. From a fine lady, Eliza has descended precipitously into a casual servant. In taking credit for her success, failing to sympathize with her plight, and calling her a presumptuous insect for daring to take credit herself, Higgins adds insult to injury.

Oddly enough, Eliza's stifled scream signals another aspect of her growing sophistication. Some months before, she would have voiced her emotions in a howl. Now the scream is but a peaking of fury. Otherwise, she expresses her feelings and her problem clearly and to the point: in short, articulately. She is quite right in calling Higgins selfish. He amply displays a self-serving lack of generosity. She is also correct in calling him a brute. This dialogue shows her more sensitive to realities than he. Most remarkably, in calling her an insect, "the creature," and a cat—cruel and imprecise name-calling, ad hominem cuts—he, for the first time, is less articulate than she. Throwing her into the easy chair substitutes brute strength for human persuasion. He momentarily wins, not on his merits, but as a bully.

When Eliza, "*crushed by his superior strength and weight*," echoes the concerns of Mrs. Pearce and Mrs. Higgins by despairing, "Whats to become of me? Whats to become of me?" Higgins's brutish reply reiterates her problem with him: "How the devil do I know whats to become of you? What does it matter what becomes of you?" Shaw accentuates another aspect of the problem when she says, "I'm nothing to you—not so much as them slippers," and Higgins, attending to her grammar, not to the aptness of her simile or her meaning, thunders, "*Those* slippers." Eliza corrects herself, again with bitter aptness: "Those slippers. I didnt think it made any difference now." When Higgins, a little uneasy with her hopelessness, returns to good humor and "*pats her kindly on the shoulder*" (as he might pat an animal), assuring her that "theres nothing more to worry about," she writhes, playing with his words: "No. Nothing more for *you* to worry about." Hiding her face, she reaches ultimate despair: "Oh God! I wish I was dead." At Higgins's declaration that "all this irritation is purely subjective," she again echoes Mrs. Pearce: "I dont understand. I'm too ignorant." And when he echoes the old Eliza—"You go to bed like a good girl and sleep it off. Have a little cry and say your prayers"—she nettles him with a wit that continues to top his: "I heard *your* prayers. 'Thank God it's all over!'" (100–101).

In this passage, Eliza develops beyond the previous one. There, irony lay in her superior articulation; here it lies most particularly in her very use of irony. Having crushed her fury, Higgins becomes condescending, but his condescension backfires as she echoes him and others. Displaying a quick ear and a sharp intellect that converts what she hears to her purposes, she deploys language ironically, outmaneuvering his superficial attempts to patch up matters. When this does not work, she tries a blunter tactic. "*Pulling herself together in desperation*," she sharply defines her problem through a staccato of questions: "What am I fit for? What have you left me fit for? Where am I to go? What am I to do? Whats to become of me?"

At last she strikes home, but only to minimal effect. Higgins, *"enlightened, but not at all impressed,"* speaks to her *"as if condescending to a trivial subject"*: "I shouldnt bother about it if I were you. I should imagine you wont have much difficulty in settling yourself somewhere or other, though I hadnt quite realized that you were going away. [*She looks quickly at him: he does not look at her, but examines the dessert stand on the piano and decides that he will eat an apple.*] You might marry, you know. [*He bites a large piece out of the apple and munches it noisily.*] You see, Eliza, all men are not confirmed old bachelors like me and the Colonel. Most men are the marrying sort (poor devils!); and youre not bad-looking: it's quite a pleasure to look at you sometimes—not now, of course, because youre crying and looking as ugly as the very devil; but when youre all right and quite yourself, youre what I should call attractive. That is, to the people in the marrying line, you understand. . . . [*he eats his apple with a dreamy expression of happiness*] . . . I daresay my mother could find some chap or other who would do very well" (102).

Higgins's nonchalant attitude about Eliza's future makes him seem far more trivial than her problem. Subtly, however, Shaw uses his condescension to lead him into an idle stream of consciousness that moves across a portion of his psychological terrain in a half-witted, self-revealing fashion. And that portion includes a pitfall he sidesteps but then teeters past unsteadily. Eliza's quick look at him when he vaguely comments, "I hadnt quite realized you were going away," registers her surprise at the prospect of staying longer, suggests that leaving is high in her mind, and responds to the wisp of a possibility that Higgins might actually regret her departure. His mention of marriage immediately after this, when he decides to eat an apple, jostles a tender subject ambiguously: ostensibly, marriage offers her an option, but covertly and dauntingly, it offers him one too. His biting and munching a large piece out of the apple just at this point gives both the audience and Higgins a pause to absorb the ambiguity. The pause is enough for him, if not for the audience. For the first time to her, he expresses his "confirmed old" bachelorhood and his pity for those who marry—his "confirmed" and "old" both defensively separating him from her. Yet grammatical slips suggest that he may be ever so slightly unhinged. His reference to bachelors "like me and the Colonel" uses *like* colloquially and, less excusably, inverts "the Colonel and I" because he is thinking first of himself. Were Eliza to slip similarly during a lesson, he would no doubt correct her, while Pickering might gently advise her that ladies do not bite large pieces out of apples and munch them noisily. More obvious unhingement appears in Higgins's flux between attraction and repulsion in what follows: "It's quite a pleasure to look at you sometimes," but not now, because crying makes her ugly; "but when youre all right and quite yourself, youre what I should call attractive. That is, to the people in the marrying line, you understand."

Shaw supplements this ambiguous self-revelation colorfully and ironically by having Higgins select the apple out of the dessert dish from which he took a chocolate to tempt Eliza in act 2, pledging his "good faith" to her by eating half of it himself before popping the other half into her mouth. Mrs. Pearce, we may recall, admonished him: "Mr Higgins: youre tempting the girl" (44–45). Both there and here, the stage property provides symbolic wit. There, like a naive Eve biting fruit from a tree of knowledge, Eliza fell for Higgins's temptations. Here, the tempter, ruminating about another pledge—marriage—uses the term "devil," as he does seven times in this short act. This devil is not only tempted by fruit from the dish (tree) that led to Eliza's fall but gobbles it (as Shaw once declared that he himself would have done if given the chance in Eden) dreamily, happily. Significantly, Higgins takes his first big bite out of the apple upon saying, "You might marry, you know," then, after "know" has rung for several moments while he munches noisily, wavers from personal denial to attraction to repulsion to attraction to avoidance, at last settling possibilities for Eliza away from himself and onto his mother finding "some chap or other" (that is, some other chap) for her.

The dodging tempter, however, is taken up short by Eliza's response: "We were above that at the corner of Tottenham Court Road." He wakes up: "What do you mean?" Her wit is more agile and deeper than his: "I sold flowers. I didnt sell myself. Now youve made a lady of me I'm not fit to sell anything else." This remark forcefully reveals how sophisticated the "good girl" has become. Her articulation is as sharp as her point. Higgins's assumption that his mother can find a chap for her reflects the genteel white slave market of Victorian times (perhaps inferred in Doolittle's attempt to "sell" Eliza to Higgins for £5), a social market in which dutiful parents sought to marry their daughters to rich or titled males. Unexpectedly foiled, *"slinging the core of the apple decisively into the grate,"* the tempter tries a different tack: "Tosh, Eliza. Dont you insult human relations by dragging all this cant about buying and selling into it. . . . What about your old idea of a florist's shop? Pickering could set you up in one. . . . I must clear off to bed: I'm devilish sleepy" (102–3). Unaware that he is hardly one to speak of human relations, he skips past her point that the marital arrangement he has offered would debase her, then contradicts his disparagement of her for calling it buying and selling when he suggests a flower shop instead. With the hour and Eliza taking their toll, he is about to retire like a weary devil.

The professor remains insensitive to the surprising fact that rhetorical victories up to this point have increasingly been Eliza's. From his point of view, he has tamed her animalistic rage, talked good sense, and congenially offered her options. Time for bed? The devil it is. Eliza, down and almost out so far as he is concerned, comes up with a final masterstroke. To penetrate his thick skull and shake his complacency, she makes her plight dramatically graphic. Playing a role that highlights the disparity between her ladylike attainments and her lower-class status, she addresses him in the manner of an underling, but pugilistically, first jolting him with, "Before you go, sir—," followed by a left hook—"Do my clothes belong to me or to Colonel Pickering?"—by another—"He might want them for the next girl you pick up to experiment on"—and another—"All I want to know is whether anything belongs to me"—then a right slammer—"I dont want to be accused of stealing." Progressively punch-drunk, Higgins reels from shock and hurt to *"deeply wounded"*: "Stealing! You shouldnt have said that, Eliza. That shews a want of feeling." *Feeling?* This from a monster who has scorned her feelings from the very first? She reminds him of society's rules: "I'm sorry. I'm only a common ignorant girl; and in my station I have to be careful. There cant be any feelings between the like of you and the like of me. Please will you tell me what belongs to me and what doesnt?" (103–4).

Readers can follow the care Shaw takes to complement the words of this scene with stage directions that modulate and build its emotions and action, much as a composer provides notations in a musical score. These are as essential as the words themselves to the dramatic and comic effects he aims at. Higgins now evolves from "*deeply wounded*" to "*very sulky*" as he declares, "You may take the whole damned houseful if you like. Except the jewels. Theyre hired. Will that satisfy you?"— then "*turns on his heel and is about to go in extreme dudgeon*" when Eliza, "*drinking in his emotion like nectar, and nagging him to provoke a further supply*," halts him with a defiant, insolent command—"Stop, please"—and takes off her jewels: "Will you take these to your room and keep them safe? I dont want to run the risk of their being missing." Her attack flourishes as Higgins, now "*furious*," commands (needlessly): "Hand them over. . . . If these belonged to me instead of to the jeweller, I'd ram them down your ungrateful throat." Apparently, neither she nor Shaw feels a need to remind him that he could take a prize for ungratefulness. This would impede the humor and pace of her vengeance, which Shaw abets without words by having Higgins thrust the jewels into his pockets, "*unconsciously decorating himself with the protruding ends of the chains.*"

As though to take Higgins up on his threat, Eliza takes off a ring: "This ring isnt the jeweller's: it's the one you bought me in Brighton. I dont want it now." When "*Higgins dashes the ring violently into the fireplace, and turns on her so threateningly that she crouches*," exclaiming, "Dont you hit me," she has him in the self-revealed, brutish position she wants him. Struck by a humiliating flash, he understands: "Hit you! You infamous creature, how dare you accuse me of such a thing? It is you who have hit me. You have wounded me to the heart." Now she uses his words and emotion to drive her wounded feelings (and possibly her heart?) home to him: "I'm glad. Ive got a little of my own back, anyhow."

How should an actress deliver this speech? It might be expressed vitriolically, bitterly, breathlessly, or with the sparkle of a tear.

Desiring not to turn this climactic moment in such dour directions but into a type of triumph, Shaw specifies that Eliza is *"thrilling with hidden joy."*

Continuing to coordinate stage directions and dialogue for maximum effects, Shaw tops this emotional climax with a brilliant comic one. While Eliza's lower-class role-playing has goaded Higgins to the brink of violence, he has been visually compromised by the jewelry protruding from his pockets, and emotionally undercut by her nettling and final joy. Now Shaw has him assuming a role opposite from hers. Higgins shifts from fury, through wounded feelings, to *"dignity, in his finest professional style,"* with a solemn falseness that comically punctures him: "You have caused me to lose my temper: a thing that has hardly ever happened to me before. I prefer to say nothing more tonight. I am going to bed." Notably, when Eliza thrilled in getting back at him, she moved from her subservient role to an equal one and a personal triumph. Now she is anything but subservient. *"Pertly"* harking back to his over-the-shoulder order to her early in the act, she declares: "Youd better leave a note for Mrs Pearce about the coffee; for she wont be told by me." His manner and his matter become increasingly incongruous as he begins, *"formally"* (still decorated by the jewelry): "Damn Mrs Pearce; and damn the coffee; and damn you; and"—then, unable to restrain himself, explodes *"wildly"*—"Damn my own folly in having lavished my hard-earned knowledge and the treasure of my regard and intimacy on a heartless guttersnipe." Final shifts add increments to the comedy as *"he goes out with impressive decorum, and spoils it by slamming the door savagely"* (104–5).

While this is the end of Higgins for the act, it leaves Eliza onstage, and Shaw could hardly drop the curtain with her just standing there. So he converts the problem into a bonus by providing a brief pantomime. Curiously, however, the bonus itself poses a problem. There are two versions of it. The original, published in 1916:

> *Eliza smiles for the first time; expresses her feelings by a wild pantomime in which an imitation of Higgins's exit is confused with her own triumph; and finally goes down on her knees on the hearthrug to look for the ring.*

Act 4: The Dark Night of Eliza's Soul

And our version, the "definitive text" of 1941:

> *Eliza goes down on her knees on the hearthrug to look for the ring.*
> *When she finds it she considers for a moment what to do with it.*
> *Finally she flings it down on the dessert stand and goes upstairs in*
> *a tearing rage.*

Our version is virtually the same length as the first one but omits
Eliza's smile and her mocking, triumphal pantomime of Higgins's exit,
converting the original ending to a first sentence, followed by Eliza
finding the ring, considering it, flinging it on the dessert stand, and
leaving in a rage.

Why worry about this detail? First, because on stage the act's
ending sets a memorable context and mood for the next act. Since the
earlier version presents Shaw's original intention for the stage, perhaps
directors should consider it. At least they should know about it.
Second, Eliza's imitation of Higgins in the earlier version is consistent
with what we know about her mimicking talents. Third, the earlier
version is more congruous with Eliza's having thrilled with hidden joy
at Higgins's discomfort and with her subsequent pert response to him.
Fourth, her smile in the earlier version ostensibly springs from joy and
triumph, but it may also suggest the warmth of fuller understanding.
These qualities contrast with the tearing rage that ends the second version and link more closely with the Eliza we shall see in act 5. Fifth,
besides being far better humored than the second version, the earlier
one is more ambiguous and potentially romantic. Eliza's search for the
ring at its end suggests a sentimental attachment. Here is a touch of
Cinderella, fittingly back among cinders, seeking an object that commonly symbolizes love. What will she do when she finds it? Throw it
away? So far as romantics are concerned, not bloody likely.

This last, no doubt, accounts for Shaw's revision. Bedeviled by
romantics who persisted in their view that Higgins should marry Eliza,
he was torpedoing evidence they might muster. Besides, Eliza's departure in a rage in the second version relates better to a subsequent scene
he added for the film. Torpedoes often miss their mark, however, and
so may this one. After all, in both versions Higgins has bought Eliza

the ring, and it obviously means something to her whether or not she flings it on the dessert stand.

Happily, readers and directors have a choice. Perhaps best of all, there is even an option for the indecisive: Shaw could have conflated the two texts in this manner:

> *Eliza smiles for the first time; expresses her feelings by a wild pantomime in which an imitation of Higgins's exit is confused with her own triumph; and finally goes down on her knees on the hearthrug to look for the ring. When she finds it she considers for a moment what to do with it. Finally she flings it down on the dessert stand and goes upstairs in a tearing rage.*

Obviously, Shaw did not choose this conflation. But such a version would combine the greater ambiguity and craft of the middle-aged playwright with the more overtly antiromantic intentions of the elderly one. It would also nicely dramatize Eliza's humor and talents as a mimic, on the one hand, and her thoughtful and feisty side, on the other. Moreover, it would double the dessert-dish symbol with the romantic symbol of the ring, as Eliza throws down another of Higgins's temptations. And it could make her consideration of what to do with the ring more ambiguous. The extreme change in mood between the smile that starts the first text and the "tearing rage" that ends the second might call for a modification. To rationalize an adjustment, one could exercise a little poetic license (as Higgins often does): "tearing" is ambiguous. It means (1) causing continued or repeated pain or distress; (2) hasty, violent; (3) splendid (chiefly British usage). If we extend (1) in a punning sense (which may have occurred to Shaw), we come close to "tearful" or "teary," either of which would temper the shift in mood. A tearful rage could naturally devolve from Eliza's smile and her consideration of the ring.[1]

In any case, the remarkable dynamics of the rest of the act would remain the same: the initial contrast between the slightly tipsy, chatty men and the almost tragic, silent Eliza; the despair of a greatly matured Eliza when she intimately experiences the forebodings of

Act 4: The Dark Night of Eliza's Soul

Mrs. Pearce and Mrs. Higgins, finding herself bleakly alone and adrift between the lower classes and the higher ones; Eliza's rejection of Cinderella dreams, in contrast to Higgins's vain Pygmalion presumption; the contention between the agony of her understanding and his egotistical indifference to it; their physical clash, his overpowering her, and his genial complacency afterward, countered by her outstripping him at his own rhetorical game and turning the tables on him, at last driving him, comically chastened, into a rage.

A perversely appealing aspect of Eliza and Higgins's contention is a sense that it could amount to a type of lovers' quarrel, starting with Eliza's depression and fury, developing through Higgins's shifts between attraction and retreat when he introduces the idea of marriage, and pivoting finally upon a ring as she, apparently treasuring it, returns it to him, saying, "I dont want it now," whereupon he throws it down, soon calling her "a heartless guttersnipe," and she at last retrieves it. This sequence offers glimpses of a romantic attraction between them for the first time. Yet romantic promise in these glimpses seems remote. The blaze of Eliza's Cinderella triumph has turned to ashes; this Cinderella's sense of self-creation has crashed against Pygmalion's sense of having created her, and in stark contrast to Cinderella's prince and Pygmalion, Higgins avoids wedlock as though it were hemlock. Thus, the Cinderella and Pygmalion mirrors in the play have shattered.

The destruction, of course, is highly intentional on Shaw's part. Patterns of the fairy tale and the myth give *Pygmalion* appealing echoes, but the play gains aesthetic power as much by countering these famous fantasies as by reflecting them. Shaw develops a profounder metaphoric pattern than romantic love in this act as Eliza, realizing the depths of her soul in darkness and despair, finds a voice within herself to articulate—partly through means that Higgins has provided—a keen awareness of her being and realities. In this self-realization, she moves beyond her tests at Mrs. Higgins's and the embassy. Those involved a contrived veneer, no matter how much she found glory in them. Now she confronts a traumatic crisis that engages her far more profoundly than anything so far.

Viewed in terms of the play as a whole, this crisis is a crucial stage in a pattern of stages through which Eliza grows, act by act. Chapter titles have signaled these:

Act 1: "Eliza's Awakening"—After Higgins refers to her soul and the divine gift of articulate speech, Eliza's attention is caught by his boast that he could make her a lady. Coins from him suddenly spur joy and exaltation in her: her dreams may become heavenly realities.

Act 2: "Purgation"—Caught up in manifold illusions about gentility, Eliza learns how imperfect and far from it she is, and submits to the painful effort of lessons that may bridge her distance from it.

Act 3: "Illumination"—Detached from her mundane background by her newly genteel appearance and language, Eliza basks sunnily in the transcendent order of Mrs. Higgins's flat yet clearly needs more expert training before she can truly rise to upper-class society.

Act 4: "The Dark Night of Eliza's Soul"—Experiencing terribly how shallow her social illumination has been, Eliza suffers an intense sense of isolation that chastens her ego, destroys her happiness, and renders her passive until Higgins sparks her fury and she cannily goads his, revealing how greatly she has grown.

We observed in chapter 3 that Pygmalion's most acute critics have sensed Eliza's growth in terms of soul but are vague about just how her soul grows. This outline suggests an answer. From a strictly secular perspective, Eliza dramatizes an eager learner evolving through progressive stages of education: first she experiences an enthusiastic "awakening" to bright possibilities; then the "purgation" of overcoming her ignorance and submitting to training; then the optimism of "illumination," the glory of having learned lessons and passed tests; but after this the sobering awareness that a good student's talents and success with tests often fail to synchronize with or answer to life's realities.

Hence, by act 4, Shaw has traced Eliza's evolution step by step, act by act, according to a worldly pattern of education. More tellingly, however, he has also linked this pattern to the growth of Eliza's soul, much as Higgins links phonetics and social concerns to matters of soul. Shaw's seriousness in depicting this evolution may be gleaned from a lecture on "Modern Religion" that he delivered in London at the time he was writing *Pygmalion*: "What I mean by a religious person is one who conceives himself or herself to be the instrument of some purpose in the universe which is a high purpose, and is the native power of evolution—that is, of a continual ascent in organization and power and life, and extension of life. . . . What I want to do is to make people more and more conscious of their souls."[2]

Just a year before he composed this lecture and *Pygmalion*, Shaw had declared, "I am, and always have been, a mystic,"[3] and in that same year, a classic work by Evelyn Underhill, titled *Mysticism*, appeared. The coincidence would be negligible were it not for the fact that, act by act, Eliza's growth relates curiously to a central passage in *Mysticism*. Underhill introduces her book's second section, "The Mystic Way," by drawing a "composite portrait" of mystics as a useful standard for viewing phases in their growth. "The first thing we notice," she comments, "is that the typical mystic seems to move towards his [or her] goal through a series of strongly marked oscillations between 'states of pleasure' and 'states of pain.'" Individual mystics obviously vary, yet taken all together, their experiences "constitute phases in a single process of growth; involving the movement of consciousness from lower to higher levels of reality, the steady remaking of character."

This last could well apply to Eliza's most significant growth in *Pygmalion* as she repeatedly oscillates between pleasure and pain. More striking, however, is the fact that so many details of Eliza's evolution resemble details in Underhill's depiction of "the Mystic Way." Underhill finds that mystics commonly evolve through five phases. Here are the first four as she summarizes them:

(1) [*Awakening:*] The awakening of the Self to consciousness of Divine Reality. This experience, usually abrupt and well-marked, is accompanied by intense feelings of joy and exaltation.

(2) [*Purgation:*] The Self, aware for the first time of Divine Beauty, realizes by contrast its own finiteness and imperfection, the manifold illusions in which it is immersed, the immense distance which separates it from the One. Its attempts to eliminate [the distance] constitute *Purgation*: a state of pain and effort.

(3) [*Illumination:*] When by Purgation the Self has become detached from the 'things of sense,' and acquired those virtues which

are the 'ornaments of the spiritual marriage,' its joyful consciousness of the Transcendent Order returns in an enhanced form. . . . Now it looks upon the sun. This is *Illumination*: a state which includes . . . training devised by experts which will strengthen and assist the mounting soul.

(4) [*The Dark Night of the Soul*:] [This is] the most terrible of all the experiences of the Mystic Way. . . . The consciousness which had, in Illumination, sunned itself in the sense of the Divine Presence, now suffers under an equally intense sense of the Divine Absence . . . now the purifying process is extended to the very center of I-hood, the will. The human instinct for personal happiness must be killed. . . . The Self now surrenders itself, [and becomes] utterly passive.[4]

Of course, Eliza is not on Underhill's "Mystic Way." Rather, she seeks personal and social self-realization. Nor does she surrender selfhood in act 4; rather, she increasingly asserts it. Yet if one compares her profoundest evolution in the play's first four acts with Underhill's first four phases of mystical evolution, graphic parallels spring forth. Shaw even renders the atmosphere and settings of each act in ways that relate to Underhill's phases as well as Eliza's. We have observed how he introduces Eliza's awakening in act 1 with divine portents in heavenly lightning, references to "soul" and a "divine gift," and the striking of a church clock, all complemented by the shelter of a church portico whose columns stand forth in the darkness. Then, too, Eliza's experiences in act 2 are set in a drawing room whose purgatorial aspects are accentuated by a lack of visible windows, the ponderous darkness of a grand piano, Piranesi engravings, and phonetics paraphernalia evoking shades of Dr. Frankenstein's laboratory. By contrast, her illumination in act 3 occurs in Mrs. Higgins's airy, elegant flat, which has three large, open windows leading to a balcony overlooking a river-and-park view, and if the embassy scene is presented, its setting is spacious and brightly lighted for the reception. In yet another contrast, Eliza's dark night of the soul in act 4 starts with Higgins's drawing room laboratory dark and peopleless. No fire lights the grate, and a clock strikes midnight before Eliza crosses to turn on lights, whereupon she sits next to the grand piano, whose darkness corresponds to her mood.

There is no proof that Shaw read Underhill's *Mysticism*, but he well may have, or he may have heard about it. His wife, mother, and sister were caught up in spiritualism and kindred subjects. Besides including religious matters in many of his plays, he identified several of his characters (as well as himself) as mystics, having created a personal religion of the "Life Force," in which he identified God with the evolution of life. Shaw's sense of a life force would resolve what might seem to be the greatest disparity between Eliza's dark night of the soul and its passive nature in Underhill's mystics—her rise beyond their passivity to effective, spirited self-assertion. Eliza is in fact passive during much of act 4, until Higgins's callousness brings out her defiant, newly effective spirit, a spirit whose growth, in Shaw's view, reflects a principle of divinity within her. What is more, she puts down a proud, conniving, self-serving creature whom Shaw repeatedly associates, however playfully, with the devil.

If Shaw knew of Underhill's book, his dramatic rendition of its principal pattern amounts to an ingenious adaptation. If he did not know it, his parallels with its carefully worked analysis reveal his sensitivity to a pattern of growth that mystics embody to an extreme degree. In addition to those who rigorously pursue education, persons who aim at exalted goals may often progress through sequences and degrees of awakening, purgation, illumination, and dispiritedness on the way to their ends. Yet Eliza's growth is extraordinary. On the one hand, her way resembles that of Underhill's mystics, set as it is in a context of divinity, myth, temptations, and soul, and presenting similar stepping-stones toward spirit. On the other hand, her aspirations, being primarily personal and social, are obviously not as ambitious as theirs, though Higgins gives her growth a spiritual slant.

Shaw fuses these similarities and differences by demonstrating how personal and social aspirations may in fact be spiritual if they involve, in Underhill's words (which could be Shaw's), "the movement of consciousness from lower to higher levels of reality, the steady remaking of character." As he shows how Eliza's growth involves such a process and leads to such ends, he presents a parable that is spiritual as well as social. The more intimate and homely a parable, the more likely that it will drive home its point. This is the case with *Pygmalion*.

Underhill continues her portrait of mystics with a final phase:

(5) [*Union*:] The true goal of the mystic quest. In this state the Absolute Life is not merely perceived and enjoyed by the Self, as in Illumination: but is *one* with it. This is the end towards which all the previous oscillations of consciousness have tended. It is a state of equilibrium, of purely spiritual life; characterized by peaceful joy, by enhanced powers, by intense certitude.

How near to this may Eliza come? Shaw presents a version of it in act 5. But for the film of the play he first inserted an overtly romantic sequence.

*   *   *

Of all the interludes, this one seems most attuned to filming: it moves Eliza from her upstairs room to outside the house, then from one London square to another, where a taxi appears. Shaw includes it primarily to forward Freddy as a romantic alternative to Higgins, an option that, to his regret, he had failed to dramatize forcefully in his original stage version.

In contrast to Eliza's room in Angel Court at the end of act 1, with its "*irreducible minimum of poverty's needs*," including a gas lamp lighted by a penny in a meter and "*a wretched bed heaped with all sorts of coverings that have any warmth in them*," Shaw specifies that her room in Wimpole Street (since we saw it in her bathing scene) "*has been increased by a big wardrobe and a sumptuous dressing table*." And in contrast to the shawl and skirt that she added to the bedclothes before she kicked off her shoes and climbed into bed in her Angel Court room, now she pulls forth a walking dress, hat, and pair of shoes before carefully adjusting her evening dress on a padded hanger and placing it in the wardrobe. Her current needs, obviously, are more psychological than material. She slams the wardrobe door and moves with "*furious resolution*"; informally but fashionably dressed to the last detail, she looks at herself in the mirror, whereupon "*she suddenly puts out her tongue at herself; then leaves the room*" (105). Thus, the flower girl defiantly scorns the fashionable lady she had once desired to be. By specifying distinctive walking attire, however, Shaw signals not only her gentility but the fact that "Walk! Not bloody likely" is far behind her: her dignity is no longer threatened by a lower-class necessity.

Act 4: The Dark Night of Eliza's Soul

When, to her surprise, she meets Freddy outside and he admits that he happily spends most of his nights there, then calls her "Miss Doolittle," Eliza's response puts her in her current no-woman's-land between the past and the present: "Liza's good enough for me." She breaks down, echoing Higgins's last words to her, showing how deeply they cut and suggesting touches of a lovers' quarrel in the preceding scene: "Freddy: you dont think I'm a heartless guttersnipe, do you?" His words, "Oh no, no, darling. . . . You are the loveliest, dearest—," followed by his smothering kisses upon one *"hungry for comfort,"* now give us romance with *heartthrobs.* Moreover, when a constable interrupts them and the lovers flee to Cavendish Square, with Eliza saying she had intended to jump into the river but that "it doesnt matter now. Theres nobody in the world now but you and me, is there?" Freddy's response, "Not a soul," gives her a soul quite different from the one Higgins said he had created, whereupon they embrace again, only to be chased off by another constable (106–8).

At last Eliza has found a companion to share her suspension between the upper and lower classes. And here is physical contact, the heat of *love* in the night. Rather vapid and banal perhaps, but who could wish for anything more? The audience? What more?

In using the arrival of a taxi to abort their embrace in yet another square, Shaw dramatically points up the change that has occurred between the Eliza of previous acts and this one. Here, the taximan asks Freddy, "Can I drive you and the lady anywhere, sir?" to which she, not Freddy, responds, "Oh, Freddy, a taxi. The very thing." Not the very thing for him: the poor gentleman has no money; but the former flower girl has a superfluity of Pickering's, so they can ride about all night before she consults with Mrs. Higgins in the morning. Besides, she comments, "the police wont touch us" in the cab (109–10). So now a taxi is for use, not for fairy-tale dreams or show or gentility, and the "lady" is happy to pay. With no concern about extravagance, she is free to snuggle and love anonymously, away from the nuisance of constables, who formerly were the Law that threatened a "good girl's" honor.

8

Act 5: Union

Much as he opened act 4 in "Cinderella" fashion with Higgins's mantel clock striking twelve, Shaw starts act 5 with an echo of a later episode in the fairy tale. Like Cinderella, Eliza has fled after midnight, on foot, with her clothing transformed. Now, like Cinderella's prince, Higgins is avidly searching her out, putting authorities on her trail. Oddly, he seems even younger than the prince. He has come running to his mother much like a thwarted, agitated child. At the rise of the curtain, a parlormaid announces to Mrs. Higgins: "Mr Henry, maam, is downstairs with Colonel Pickering. . . . Telephoning to the police, I think . . . in a state, maam." Sitting at her writing table, resembling a cool, collected parent used to tantrums, the lady responds, "If you had told me that Mr Henry was not in a state it would have been more surprising. . . . I suppose he's lost something." Her "some*thing*" turns out to be prescient, since she soon scolds Higgins and Pickering: "What right have you to go to the police and give the girl's name as if she were a thief, or a lost umbrella, or something? Really! . . . You have no more sense, either of you, than two children" (111–13). The children appear to have lost not just a subject but an object.

Act 5: Union

Before the males enter, we discover that women have formed a tacit alliance to handle them. Mrs. Higgins tells the maid to "go upstairs and tell Miss Doolittle that Mr Henry and the Colonel are here. Ask her not to come down til I send for her," and when Higgins bursts in to inform her that Eliza has bolted—"She came in a cab for her things before seven this morning; and that fool Mrs Pearce let her have them without telling me a word about it"—we see that the alliance includes his housekeeper as well as his mother, the maid, and Eliza. Mrs. Higgins's identification of Eliza as "Miss Doolittle," in contrast to the name both she and the maid use for Higgins, "Mr Henry," incidentally suggests that while Eliza is to be treated as a lady, Higgins demonstrates that men will be boys.

Like a naughty son, Higgins conceals the truth from his mother when she says that he must have frightened Eliza: "Frightened her! nonsense! She was left last night, as usual, to turn out the lights and all that; and instead of going to bed she changed her clothes and went right off. . . . What am I to do?" His "as usual" witlessly gives away his treatment of Eliza as a servant, and when Mrs. Higgins puts him down, as a good mother should ("Do without, I'm afraid, Henry. The girl has a perfect right to leave if she chooses"), his distracted response reveals that he has used the girl as a secretary too: "But I cant find anything. I dont know what appointments Ive got." Unaware that his fretting, much like a child's, shows every concern for himself and none for Eliza, his telephoning the police turns this boy into an ominous adult who reflects the Law much as he had to the flower girl in act 1. His mother, deeply vexed, is about to chastise the boys when Shaw overlaps this action with the maid's announcement of a gentleman—a Mr. Doolittle—who wants to see Higgins.

The interruption is dramatically charged. The fact that we know Eliza is upstairs and Higgins and Pickering do not gives tension to the scene, tends to identify us with Mrs. Higgins's secret, and whets our appetite for what will happen when the two searchers find out. Just as it seems that they are about to, our suspense is tantalizingly suspended and compounded by Doolittle's arrival. We look forward to the interruption because its surprise returns us to the wonderful World of Alfred, which we last witnessed in act 2. Like that diversion, this one adds color to the act and comically seasons the play with perspectives that reflect upon the main action. In act 2 we had the quirky contrast between Eliza's fervent sense of morality and her father's frank immorality, she feeling and thinking herself deserving, he rationalizing and relishing himself as undeserving. Now Shaw presents us not just with a contrast but also with quirky similarity: Eliza's social rise is matched by her father's, and Shaw uses Doolittle's loquaciousness to explore different aspects of their success.

What makes a man, his speech or his clothes? Shaw puts Higgins's priorities to another test. Mrs. Pearce, we may recall, put Alfred down in act 2 by introducing him merely as "Doolittle." Because of his garb? Most likely. Now when Pickering questions whether this is the dustman, the parlormaid responds, "Dustman! Oh no, sir: a gentleman." Servants should know: two votes against phonetics. Shaw has given Eliza many transformations in appearance: from a flower girl to a flower girl pretentiously dolled up in a great feather hat, to an exotic maiden in a kimono who dons the feather hat, to a stunning lady in an afternoon dress, then in an evening dress, then in walking attire—each an impressive change suggesting her evolution. Doolittle's sartorial shift, by contrast, comes with a bang. Transformed from the grubbiest of the low to a peak of the high, he appears *"resplendently dressed as for a fashionable wedding,"* including *"a dazzling silk hat, and patent leather shoes"* (113). In itself, this radical change evokes a comic effect. Why is it that a sudden, astonishing improvement in a man's appearance may provoke comedy more than a similar one in a woman? Perhaps because hope springs eternal that latent beauty in a woman may suddenly flower. In any event, for the former dustman, this comic twist becomes the first of many.

Doolittle shows his rough background when he forgets his hostess in his vehement desire to reproach Higgins, then reveals a touch of native gentility when he apologizes to her for doing so. He accosts the professor for an incongruous reason, gesturing at his own incongruously impressive attire: "See here! Do you see this? *You* done this." Higgins, his mind elsewhere, prompts another twist: "Have you found Eliza?" "Have you lost her?" "Yes." "You have all the luck, you have." And Mrs. Higgins spins off yet another: "But what has my son done to you, Mr Doolittle?" "Done to me! Ruined me. Destroyed my happiness. Tied me up and delivered me into the hands of middle class morality" (113–15). The accursed propriety the dustman inveighed against in act 2 has seized him, throwing him topsy-turvy.

Doolittle's explanation that Higgins has led to this deplorable situation by recommending him as "the most original moralist at present in England" to an American millionaire who was founding moral reform societies all over the world is punctured when Higgins calls it a silly joke. But the joke itself has been punctured by the millionaire's act of leaving Doolittle a large income for occasional lectures. Doolittle's plight, comically convoluted in itself, is also comically fertile. Shaw championed Henrik Ibsen as an original moralist and considered himself among the most original moralists in England. Thus, the joke jostles its writer. Beyond this lies a moral: when writing letters of recommendation, never jest: you may be taken seriously. Springing further, here we have philanthropy not just throwing money away but throwing it to one who would sabotage its goals. And beyond this irony is yet another: the millionaire has thrust an original moralist into the grimly unoriginal sphere of middle-class morality, plunging him into a life full of excruciating burdens: "Who asked him to make a gentleman of me? I was happy. I was free. . . . Now I am worrited; tied neck and heels; and everybody touches *me* for money." In the good old days, a lawyer dropped him as quickly as possible; now, doctors who used to shove him out of the hospital half-cured will not let him alone, relatives besiege him, Eliza will too, and he will have to take lessons from Higgins. But he can hardly give up the money because the prospect of an impoverished old age now intimidates him (115–17).

An irony arching above Doolittle's complaint is that Shaw uses it to make a case not against but for middle-class morality, a point he tucks briefly into Doolittle's torrent: "I have to live for others and not for myself: thats middle class morality." The virtue in this enforced altruism is not unambiguous, however. It includes worrying and responsibilities, the avarice of lawyers, a health care–less system with a hypocritic oath, a world of parasites eager for the dole—one of which, until now, he had happily been.

In a coda to Doolittle's lament, Shaw suggests a resolution to a major theme of the play, touches comically on Eliza's plight, and drives home middle-class ambiguity all at the same time. Mrs. Higgins observes that "this solves the problem of Eliza's future. You can provide for her now," to which Doolittle responds, "[*with melancholy resignation*] Yes, maam: I'm expected to provide for everyone now, out of three thousand a year." His acquiescence spurs Higgins to jump up: "Nonsense! . . . She doesnt belong to him. I paid him five pounds for her. Doolittle: either youre an honest man or a rogue." The newly burdened middle-class soul "*tolerantly*" reveals his dustman's honesty and insight by replying, "A little of both, Henry, like the rest of us: a little of both." Tolerance of life's changes and ambiguities, Shaw often stressed, offers a key to progress.

Higgins himself shows little tolerance when his mother reveals that Eliza is upstairs and has told her of the men's brutality. Pickering protests, but then turns on his friend, knowing his man: "Higgins: did you bully her after I went to bed?" The professor, who is now sitting because his mother ordered him to, gives a "I-didn't-hit-her-she-hit-me" response: "She threw my slippers in my face." His intuitive mother then introduces a view of Eliza that only Freddy seems to have had so far: "The girl is naturally rather affectionate, I think. . . . She had become attached to you both." Mrs. Higgins details their indifference to Eliza after her success at the embassy ("she did this wonderful thing for you without making a single mistake"), revealing how much Eliza has told her and how much she understands: "Then you were surprised because she threw your slippers at you! *I* should have thrown the fire-irons at you." When she censures the men's failure to thank or tell Eliza how splendid she had been, Higgins's impatient response exposes a root of the problem: "But she knew all about that. We didnt make speeches to her, if thats what you mean" (118–19).

So far in this act, the two persons who have said "I think" are women, the parlormaid and Mrs. Higgins, a detail that reflects back to act 3, where both Higgins and Pickering repeat Mrs. Pearce's admonition to them: "You dont think, sir." Consistent in their witlessness, the men are still not thinking. Trying to jog them, Mrs. Higgins has briefly and clearly articulated perceptions, feelings, points of view, understandings, and backgrounds of the situation, and has been genteel and tactful in doing so. She has given the lie to her son's narrowly one-sided account of Eliza's slipper toss yet, rather than call him mendacious, has artfully expanded the frame of reference to show him his insensitivity. Still, knowing Henry's self-centered deafness, she has then whopped him with a graphic rhetorical conclusion: she would have thrown not his slippers but the fire irons at him. She may even be wittily alluding to his stumbling over her fire irons in act 3, another instance of his social clumsiness.

Higgins's response reveals obstinate insularity both to her subtlety and to her rhetorical fire irons. "We didnt make speeches to her, if thats what you mean" not only misses her sensitivity and frame of reference but defies them and, like a peevish child, does so inaccurately. A "speech," of course, is the opposite of the courtesy and consideration she is urging. Eliza ran into similar thickheadedness when she confronted him in act 4. She was nearly as articulate there as his mother is here, but could not be as sustained in expressing herself because her tumultuous feelings and his insensitive responses got in the way.

Although Higgins scarcely hears his mother, Pickering finally does and begins to understand. His *"conscience stricken"* comment—"Perhaps we were a little inconsiderate. Is she very angry?"—gives Mrs. Higgins a small bridge across the gully between Eliza and the men. As she has done from the beginning of the act, she stage-manages the situation, now commenting that she will ask Eliza to come down, provided Henry behaves himself, and moving Doolittle, along with the shock of his news, to the balcony. Her recalcitrant boy remains a problem, sulkily shifting blame from himself and denigrating Eliza: "Oh all right. Very well. Pick: you behave yourself. Let us put on our best Sunday manners for this creature that we picked out of the mud."

Eliza's appearance sparks a brilliant comedy of manners. It begins simply. The person Higgins has just labeled "this creature" enters, *"sunny, self-possessed, and giving a staggeringly convincing exhibition of ease of manner."* The contrast between her bright spirit, self-control, maturity, manner, and Higgins's petulance, lack of self-control, and indecorum is strikingly apparent, comic both in itself and as it whets the audience's appetite for what is to come. In many respects, their roles at this point have radically reversed the positions they held in acts 1 and 2: she is the image of gentility, he the plaintive urchin. Heightening the comedy is the sense that this is an *"exhibition."* Much as Mrs. Higgins has stage-managed, Eliza is playing a role beautifully. Conveying an impression of intimately belonging in a fine lady's quarters, *"she carries a little work-basket, and is very much at home."* She even starts conversation in a pleasant manner: "How do you do, Professor Higgins? Are you quite well?" He chokes, so she answers for him: "But of course you are: you are never ill. So glad to see you again, Colonel Pickering. . . . Quite chilly, this morning, isnt it?" Pickering, at first *"too much taken aback to rise,"* rises hastily, and they shake hands. Why has the professor choked; why is the gentleman nonplussed? Higgins commands: "Dont you dare try this game on me. I taught it to you. . . . Get up and come home; and dont be a fool" (120).

What game? The men are confounded not just by the stunning contrast between the distraught runaway they expected to find and the suavely collected lady they see before them, or by her formality in contrast to an informality familiar to them, or by her game of social manners, but specifically by her use of the game's *abcs.* Anything but a fool, Eliza is urbanely mocking Higgins with the small-talk openings about weather and health that he taught her for her test in this room in act 3. Pickering's impulse to shake hands sets the tone of a revised, more formal and equal relationship between them. Perhaps coached by Mrs. Higgins, *"Eliza takes a piece of needlework from her basket, and begins to stitch at it, without taking the least notice of* [Higgins's] *outburst."* She has apparently learned that no response can be the best response, that one can be aggressive by being passive in a testy situation. Contrary to the professor's professional bent, a well-timed silence may be articulate, and her articulation now lies in not descending to his level, in ignoring him, in stitching. She has, after all, won round one.

Mrs. Higgins rises to Eliza's defense: "Very nicely put, indeed, Henry. No woman could resist such an invitation." His rejoinder self-confidently puts his ego, his profession, and Eliza's debt to him on the line: "You let her alone, mother. Let her speak for herself. You will jolly soon see whether she has an idea that I havnt put into her head or a word that I havnt put into her mouth. I tell you I have created this thing out of the squashed cabbage leaves of Covent Garden; and now she pretends to play the fine lady with me." His mother's response— "Yes dear; but youll sit down, wont you?"—acquiesces not to his rudeness but to his blunt challenge that she let Eliza alone and let her speak for "herself": her ideas and words will be his. (Yes yes sweetheart, but why stand?) Higgins *"sits down again, savagely"* (120–21).

The floor is now open to Eliza and Pickering, and their exchange constitutes yet another major test of her. The former tests gauged her training. This one will gauge if there is any depth or originality behind her genteel facade. Now the judges are experts far beyond the Eynsford Hills or Nepommuck, and their role is to listen . . .

Suavely, Eliza acknowledges neither Higgins nor the test. She continues stitching. Yet her dialogue with Pickering reveals that she is rising to Higgins's challenge. In addressing Pickering conversationally, she gives Higgins few openings for a response while, in effect, answering him in earnest. Her tactics and language are as deft as her stitching. First she attacks his dehumanizing of her: "Will *you* drop me altogether now that the experiment is over, Colonel Pickering?" Capitalizing on Pickering's shock—"You mustnt think of it as an experiment"—she attacks Higgins's reference to her origins: "Oh, I'm only a squashed cabbage leaf . . . ," then counters Higgins's claim that he created her, giving Pickering greater credit: ". . . but I owe so much to you. . . . It was from you that I learnt really nice manners; and that is what makes one a lady, isnt it?" This leads her to identify Higgins as more a hindrance than a help: "You see it was so very difficult for me with the example of Professor Higgins always before me," whereupon she links the professor to her cabbage-leaf background: "I was brought up to be just like him, unable to control myself, and using bad language on the slightest provocation."

When Pickering tries to salvage something for his friend—"Still, he taught you to speak"—she nonchalantly trivializes phonetics: "Of course: that is his profession. . . . It was just like learning to dance in the fashionable way." In contrast, she draws forth a crucial memory: "But do you know what began my real education?" She stops her stitching for a moment, a break that emphasizes her point: "Your calling me Miss Doolittle that day when I first came to Wimpole Street.

That was the beginning of self-respect for me." Pickering's many genteel courtesies toward her, in contrast to Higgins's crude habits and behavior, followed that: "You see, really and truly, apart from the things anyone can pick up (the dressing and the proper way of speaking, and so on), the difference between a lady and a flower girl is not how she behaves, but how she's treated. I shall always be a flower girl to Professor Higgins, because he always treats me as a flower girl, and always will; but I know I can be a lady to you, because you always treat me as a lady, and always will" (121–22).

After this sophisticated demolition, one might almost pity Higgins, even though he clearly has asked for it. His self-confident request that his mother let Eliza speak for herself has devastatingly backfired. She has not only answered to his test of her depth and originality as a lady but has turned the test around to judge his own lack of gentility and converted it into a damning appraisal of his profession. In the previous act, she had his insular ego to contend with, and her wounded feelings were to the fore. Now that the kindly Pickering allows her thoughts free play, she hashes Higgins's assumption that her ideas are but a rehash of his. She has not been entirely fair, but then neither has he. Her fluent diction and language no doubt owe much to him. Yet his boast that he alone has created her and that she only pretends to be a lady crumbles in her brightly articulated sense that good manners and respect both from without and within are more essential to gentility than his phonetics.

The limits of phonetics, elegant appearance, and social manners were exposed in this room in act 3 when the mechanical doll of a lady had to rely on something other than its programming. It answered with the only human experience it had—its squalid background—and did so with colorful ingenuity. But its background nearly shattered its show. Now, laboring less on the mechanics of speech, Eliza has absorbed new contexts, and these offer her native ingenuity a new range. In an important way, the test in act 3 was a test not just of her but of Higgins's profession, one he barely passed by fudging her "small talk." Now the test pits not only his professional conceits but also his personal egotism against Eliza as a real lady, and the lady wins her greatest round hands down. The professor has flunked.

Act 5: Union

Higgins, who can only sputter "Well!!" and "Damnation!" in the course of this grinding, is apparently reflecting it when his mother comments, "Please dont grind your teeth, Henry." Eliza's intellectual triumph here matches her emotional one at the end of act 4 when she says she would now like Pickering to call her Eliza and Higgins to call her Miss Doolittle. The egotistical monster seems thoroughly one-upped, exposed, confounded, foiled: "I'll see you damned first." In response to Pickering's laughter and urging, "Why dont you slang back at him?" Eliza takes a high road: "I have forgotten my own language."

Even when merited, however, pride can be dangerous, and Shaw punctures Eliza's at its zenith by bringing in her father, whose resplendent appearance evokes one of her old howls. Grasping this straw from the jaws of defeat, Higgins crows, "Aha! Just so. A-a-a-a-ahowooh! A-a-a-a-ahowooh! A-a-a-a-ahowooh! Victory! Victory!" Were he more restrained and astute, he might better have crowed at Eliza's following deflation when, upon finding that her father is about to let himself down "to marry that low common woman," she says reluctantly that she will attend the wedding: "If the Colonel says I must, I—I'll [*almost sobbing*] I'll demean myself." More compromising to her gentility than her slip into a howl is her continuing snobbery. Both Pickering and Mrs. Higgins, far surer of their status, are going. Pickering is consistent to the end—"Before I go, Eliza, do forgive Higgins and come back to us"—and so is Doolittle: "They played you off very cunning, Eliza, them two sportsmen. If it had been only one of them, you could have nailed him. But you see, there was two; and one of them chaperoned the other. . . . It was artful of you, Colonel; but I bear no malice: I should have done the same myself" (123–25).

With the others gone and Mrs. Higgins dressing for the wedding, Eliza and Higgins are left together. Apparently desiring to address matters that are now out of hand, Higgins maneuvers his back to the door to prevent her escape. Although he spraddled arrogantly on the divan after declaring "Victory" at her howl, he is at least partly aware that the most impressive victory has been hers. She may not formally be a lady, but she has played the lady devastatingly well, far better than many real articles could, and this awareness has changed him. His tone and manner are conciliatory. Implicitly acknowledging her success, the child in him vanishes: "Well, Eliza, youve had a bit of your own back, as you call it. Have you had enough?" whereupon Eliza converts "your own back" to what is foremost in her mind and his: their future relationship: "You want me back only to pick up your slippers and put up with your tempers and fetch and carry for you." Higgins shows frank self-knowledge on one hand—"If you come back I shall treat you just as I have always treated you. I cant change my nature; and I dont intend to change my manners"—but then takes a perverse twist: "My manners are exactly the same as Colonel Pickering's." When Eliza declares, "Thats not true. He treats a flower girl as if she was a duchess," he counters, "And I treat a duchess as if she was a flower girl." "I see," she observes, "the same to everybody. . . . Like father." Higgins, *"grinning, a little taken down,"* returns: "Without accepting the comparison at all points, Eliza, it's quite true that your father is not a snob" (126).

The comparisons deftly define differences between four persons: Pickering who is courteous to all, Higgins who is courteous to few, Doolittle who naturally goes his egalitarian way between the two, and Eliza whose snobbery undercuts her. Higgins might well refer to her recent display of snobbery, but now his good humor and his desire to coax her restrain him. He even ignores her slip in "as if she was [instead of *were*] a flower girl," repeating her error himself so as not to jar her. Serious now, he confides, "The great secret, Eliza, is . . . having the same manner for all human souls: in short, behaving as if you were in Heaven, where there are no third-class carriages, and one soul is as good as another."

This earthly image, linking humanity, the soul, and heaven, introduces the flux between the mundane and the spiritual in what follows. Through their gift for articulate speech, the two illuminate primary differences in their temperaments and goals. The focus falls first on Higgins. Eliza asserts the self-respect she learned from Pickering—"I wont be passed over"—and the machine in Higgins responds, "Then get out of my way; for I wont stop for you. You talk about me as if I were a motor bus." She propels his metaphor—"So you are a motor bus: all bounce and go, and no consideration for anyone. But I can do without you"—a declaration he soon tops, only to descend precipitously in a personally telling manner:

> HIGGINS [*arrogant*] I can do without anybody. I have my own soul: my own spark of divine fire. But [*with sudden humility*] I shall miss you, Eliza. [*He sits down near her on the ottoman*] I have learnt something from your idiotic notions: I confess that humbly and gratefully. And I have grown accustomed to your voice and appearance. I like them, rather.
>
> LIZA. Well, you have both of them on your gramophone and in your book of photographs. When you feel lonely without me, you can turn the machine on. It's got no feelings to hurt.
>
> HIGGINS. I cant turn your soul on. Leave me those feelings; and you can take away the voice and the face. They are not you.
>
> LIZA. Oh, you *are* a devil. You can twist the heart in a girl as easy as some could twist her arms to hurt her. Mrs Pearce warned me. . . . You dont care a bit for me.
>
> HIGGINS. I care for life, for humanity; and you are a part of it that has come my way and been built into my house. What more can anyone ask?
>
> LIZA. I wont care for anybody that doesnt care for me.
>
> HIGGINS. Commercial principles, Eliza. Like [selling violets], isnt it? . . . I dont and wont trade in affection. (127–28)

This dialogue and much surrounding it reveal the great disparity between their attraction to one another. Their consciousness and values are on different tracks, a situation dramatically illustrating Higgins's words to Pickering in act 2 about why he finds himself incompatible with women: "Women upset everything. When you let them into your life, you find that the woman is driving at one thing and youre driving at another. . . . I suppose the woman wants to live her own life; and the man wants to live his; and each tries to drag the other on to the wrong track" (50). Beyond the grubby flower girl, she can now articulate her thoughts and feelings, and beyond the purely scientific gentleman, he now believes that he can express his to her—an implicit acknowledgment of a type of equality—but his spark of divine fire comes from a foreign sphere. Still, what has he learned from notions he calls "idiotic"? We find that she has brought him into touch with humanity, a touch that reawakens the enthusiasm for her soul that he expressed after her test in this room in act 3. Now, however, her soul and her humanity, having grown in their dark night of apprehension and self-appraisal and combat with him after the embassy reception, and through her recent expression of her debt to Pickering, are greater than he can appreciate or articulate. His designation of her notions as "idiotic" is strikingly inarticulate and evasive. It cuts him off from fully engaging her depths, attitudes, and ambivalences, her distinctive soul and humanity. What he cannot acknowledge is that, except for her snobbery, her native sophistication now comes close to his mother's, with the oblique advantage that her poverty has given her sensibilities more earthly scope.

Besides keenly parrying his lukewarm admission that he has "grown accustomed" to her voice and appearance and likes them, "rather," Eliza's comment that he can turn on the machine to hear her voice echoes his words to Pickering before she entered his laboratory in act 2: "We'll get her on the phonograph so that you can turn her on as often as you like." At that time, he had no interest in her other than as a dialect. Now his view has changed, but in a direction as spiritually abstract as it was scientifically specific then. Her remark that the machine has no feelings to hurt, and his response that his feelings for her soul are greater than his feelings for her voice and face, ironically resurrect his slighting of her feelings then. While her feelings are knotted in affection for him, he abstracts his for her as a caring for life, for humanity, reaching beyond her as a person to her soul as a part of humanity that has been intimately built into his house.

Who could ask for anything more? She does, asking for reciprocity of her affection in kind. To him, this amounts to a trading instinct much like that in commerce, a penny for a violet. He appears to perceive according to divine principles, she according to mundane ones, yet he is unaware that aspects of divinity may inform her desire.

Ironically, just when Higgins expresses spiritual sensibilities, Eliza specifically calls him a devil for the first time in the play. In accordance with his affection and values, he offers her good fellowship and considers a woman fetching a man's slippers, in contrast, disgusting, the act of a slave trying to trade in affection. In one way his ego links with her snobbery when he sets her "little dog's tricks of fetching and carrying slippers against my creation of a Duchess Eliza" (a sentiment that also pits her animalistic past against her extraordinary present). For him, the creative process has been professional and transcendent, but for her, it has been emotional and social. She asks, "What did you do it for if you didnt care for me?" He answers heartily, "Why, because it was my job," and then responds to the trouble it has caused her by linking his job to that of the world's maker: "Making life means making trouble." She tries to bring this flight to earth: "I'm no preacher: I dont notice things like that. I notice that you dont notice me." Frustrated, *"jumping up and walking about intolerantly,"* he declares, "Eliza: youre an idiot. I waste the treasures of my Miltonic mind by spreading them before you" (128).

In identifying his mind with Milton's, Higgins defines and exalts himself yet unconsciously undercuts himself and reveals much about their failure to communicate. Like Milton, his titanic ego visits high principles on the mundane and renders him intolerant of opposing views. But how may his high principles function in life? Shaw puts Higgins to a poetic test that reflects Milton and William Blake, both of whose works he knew well. As Milton presumes "to justify the ways of God to men" in *Paradise Lost*, Higgins is justifying his ways to Eliza. Blake, however, discerned that the poetic splendor with which Milton portrays Satan in *Paradise Lost* reveals that he was "of the Devil's party without knowing it."[1] Given the many parallels between Higgins and Milton, these famous words add satiric bite to Eliza's first calling Higgins a devil, then a preacher shortly afterward. Higgins is tempting her toward his own ends, and like Milton, his spirituality has a diabolical aspect as he exalts spirit over personal feeling. His position also calls up ghosts of Milton's well-known personal life: prayerfully,

Milton married the first of his three wives at the age of 33. Half his age, uneducated, and tormented by their incompatibility, the girl soon fled. Living with him was hell. The scholarly poet desired not just love but mental fellowship in marriage. In Higgins, such instincts emerge as those of a bachelor desiring "good fellowship" but evading the reciprocities of marriage.

Eliza catches sight of his dodge and shows her own instincts when she responds "*fiercely*" after Higgins offers to adopt her and asks whether she would rather marry Pickering: "I wouldnt marry *you* if you asked me; and youre nearer my age than what he is." Diverting matters from good fellowship to warmer prospects, she provokes a revealing exchange by informing him that Freddy has been writing her several times a day:

HIGGINS [*disagreeably surprised*] Damn his impudence! . . . You have no right to encourage him.

LIZA. Every girl has a right to be loved.

HIGGINS. What! By fools like that?

LIZA. Freddy's not a fool. And if he's weak and poor and wants me, may be he'd make me happier than my betters that bully me and dont want me.

HIGGINS. Can he *make* anything of you? Thats the point.

LIZA. Perhaps I could make something of him. But I never thought of us making anything of one another; and you never think of anything else. I only want to be natural. (129)

Higgins is unaware that he overreaches himself in dictating Eliza's rights just after he damns Freddy's impudence. Who is impudent here? What girl does not have a right to be loved? His calling Freddy a fool amounts to a habit pattern. As he has also applied the word to Eliza and Mrs. Pearce, it, like "idiot," lacks discrimination, rather like Eliza's howls. Now, more articulately than the professor, the former howler defines Freddy as weak and poor and in love with her, then takes an adroitly oblique tack: for all his faults, Freddy may make her happier than her bullying betters (Higgins) who don't want (love) her. Similarly, Higgins's "can he *make* anything of you" refers to himself. It is hardly *the* point: it is his point. Since Higgins has already made something of her, the former flower girl can turn his point upside down: she may be able to make something of Freddy. And contrary to Higgins, she wisely senses that intentions to "make something" of a spouse may not lead to marital happiness. Being "natural" apart from such ambitions beats their unnatural warp.

Eliza's subsequent plea—"I want a little kindness"—expresses in a moment a surer route to happiness than a lifetime's attempt to make something of someone, while her explanation of her motives and the ambiguity of her feelings during the months Higgins was making something of her takes 15 seconds: "What I done [*correcting herself*] what I did was not for the dresses and the taxis: I did it because we were pleasant together and I come—came—to care for you; not to want you to make love to me, and not forgetting the difference between us, but more friendly like" (130). Her emotion causes her grammar, syntax, and articulation to falter between her past and her present. Yet combined with her emotion, her words and stumbles deliver her thoughts and feelings succinctly and clearly.

Higgins's long response, by comparison, expresses his thoughts and feelings eloquently but misses his mark, showing how faulty eloquence can be: "If you cant stand the coldness of my sort of life, and the strain of it, go back to the gutter. . . . Oh, it's a fine life, the life of the gutter. It's real: it's warm: it's violent. . . . Not like Science and Literature and Classical Music and Philosophy and Art. You find me cold, unfeeling, selfish, dont you? Very well: . . . Marry some sentimental hog or other with lots of money, and a thick pair of lips to kiss you with and a thick pair of boots to kick you with." In contrast to her, he makes his case poorly. Posing the coldness of culture (is it cold?) against warmth in the gutter (is it warm?) on the one hand, and marriage to a rich, sentimental, gross pig on the other, his argument bypasses the obvious. It misrepresents Eliza: "You know I cant go back to the gutter. . . . You know well I couldnt bear to live with a low common man after you two." And since none of it fits Freddy, it points Eliza in the direction Higgins wants her to avoid. Boldly defying the social order of things (in those days), Eliza declares realistically, "I'll marry Freddy, I will, as soon as I'm able to support him" (130–31).

One brave idea goads another: why not support Freddy by teaching phonetics? Higgins's laughter at this could mean a dozen things, most not flattering, but his shift to fury at her following notion to assist Nepommuck puts him where she wants him. When he declares that he will wring her neck and lays hands on her, she has won her battle, as she did at the end of act 4. Combined with her declaration of independence, this is even sweeter: "Wring away. What do I care? I knew youd strike me some day." Exposed as the brute she has found this devil to be, "*he lets her go, stamping with rage at having forgotten himself, and recoils so hastily that he stumbles back into his seat on the ottoman.*" The intellectual snob is the beast now, and she the lady above him: "Aha! Now I know how to deal with you. . . . [*Purposely dropping her aitches to annoy him*] Thats done you Enry Iggins, it az. . . . Oh, when I think of myself crawling under your feet and being trampled on and called names, when all the time I had only to lift up my finger to be as good as you, I could just kick myself" (131–32).

Shaw keeps the scene at a high ironic pitch by having Higgins presumably not foiled, but rising to her triumph. Her resolute self-assertion and defiance are better than sniveling or fetching slippers: "By George, Eliza, I said I'd make a woman of you; and I have. I like you like this." To her response that he has turned around because now she can do without him, he flashes evidence that, while she has changed, he has not: "Of course I do, you little fool. Five minutes ago you were like a millstone round my neck. Now youre a tower of strength: a consort battleship. You and I and Pickering will be three old bachelors instead of only two men and a silly girl."

Typically, Higgins slants matters in his favor. He has never said that he would make a woman of Eliza. Rather, his bet with Pickering was to make a lady of her, a task he has partly accomplished. Partly, because even the mechanical lady at the start of act 3 was a composite creation of his phonetic skills, Pickering's and Mrs. Pearce's manners, and Eliza's talents and drive. After act 3, the example of Mrs. Higgins probably helped her. In this act, Eliza has credited Pickering not only as an example of good manners but also as the one who first gave her self-respect, a quality that girds her declaration of independence now. And we have seen how Eliza's tenacity and success have also come from her affection for Higgins, affection Shaw suggests in their curious lovers' quarrel in act 4. Self-respect and affection inform her contention with Higgins in this act, her evolution now being of little credit to him, except as he provides a honing counterforce. Eliza grows as a woman (not a lady) through progressively rising to and engaging this counterforce and coming to grips with alternatives—Freddy and independence. Higgins acknowledges few of these matters. For him, "I's" prevail. Once again, he takes credit only partly deserved for her creation and growth, with the self-indulgence of his "three old bachelors" declaration functioning witlessly as a prod to drive her away.

Mrs. Higgins's return to notify Eliza that the carriage is waiting gives this erstwhile Cinderella a fitting vehicle for escaping her erstwhile Pygmalion. The scene's tone changes with Eliza becoming *"instantly cool and elegant."* As a lady, she contrasts dramatically with the "woman" Higgins says he has made, but by now the woman informs the lady, rendering her gentility valid and strong.

Eliza's "Then I shall not see you again, Professor. Goodbye," has a ring of finality, while Higgins asserts the opposite by nonchalantly ordering (not requesting) her to order a ham and a cheese and buy him gloves and a tie: *"His cheerful, careless, vigorous voice shews that he is incorrigible."* Eliza *"disdainfully"* corrects the order detail by detail, a hint that while she served she also controlled. Declaring, "What you are to do without me I cannot imagine," she *"sweeps out"* (133). Mrs. Higgins's comment that "I should be uneasy about you and her if she were less fond of Colonel Pickering" is, in turn, corrected by Higgins: "Pickering! Nonsense: she's going to marry Freddy. Ha ha! Freddy! Freddy!! Ha ha ha ha ha!!!!! [*He roars with laughter as the play ends*].

*   *   *

Ultimately ironic is the fact that the play does not necessarily, conclusively, end this way. A knowing observer might ask, which play? In Shaw's original version, Eliza does not correct Higgins's order for a ham, cheese, and so forth. Rather, she *"disdainfully"* says, "Buy them yourself," then sweeps out, leaving Mrs. Higgins to comment, "I'm afraid youve spoiled that girl, Henry. But never mind, dear: I'll buy you the tie and gloves," to which he replies, "*sunnily*," "Oh, dont bother. She'll buy em all right enough. Good-bye." The final stage direction reads: "*They kiss. Mrs Higgins runs out. Higgins, left alone, rattles his cash in his pocket; chuckles; and disports himself in a highly self-satisfied manner.*"

Differences between the two versions highlight Shaw's climactic thrust against the romantics who would cling to a "Cinderella" or "Pygmalion" ending. In the original version, Eliza's "Buy them yourself" and Higgins's response to his mother, "She'll buy em all right enough," leave ambiguity, a crack in the door for romantics to pry at. In contrast, Eliza's detailing and countering his order in the later version, followed by her "What you are to do without me, I cannot imagine," coupled with Higgins's emphatic declaration to his mother that "she's going to marry Freddy. Ha ha! Freddy! Freddy!!" has Shaw pounding the audience with her decision at the curtain. Which is best? Perhaps the original, more ambiguous ending, since a mature audience would have to mull the matter. Yet Shaw found mature audiences in short supply. That is why he changed the text. Besides, the later ending is more dynamic. It makes for a better curtain. One may choose.

More extreme alternatives exist. First is Shaw's actual film script for the play (as opposed to our edited version), in which Freddy thanks Higgins for setting Eliza and himself up in a flower shop: "Her old dream, you know. A lady in a flower shop"—dissolving to Eliza in the past: "Poor girl! . . . Let him mind his own business and leave a poor girl alone"—dissolving into a vision of the future: "*A florist's shop . . . full of fashionable customers. Liza behind the counter, serving in great splendor. The name of the shopkeeper, F. HILL, is visible*"—with a fade-out to Mrs. Higgins's garden gate, where Higgins, at first "*standing rapt,*" comments to a concerned policewoman: "No: Nothing wrong. A happy ending. A happy beginning. Good morning, madam."[2] Directors of the Oscar-winning film concocted three different endings, finally settling on one in which Higgins returns home, plays a record of Eliza's voice, and switches it off, whereupon Eliza herself returns, saying she has washed her face and hands (as she said when she first came to Wimpole Street). With self-confident pleasure, Higgins asks for his slippers—followed by studio music rising to the sentimentally happy END. Two more choices! or three, with *My Fair Lady*. But only the first is Shaw's.

9

The End

Shaw's afterword, in which Eliza marries Freddy and, aided by Pickering and Higgins, opens a flower and greengrocer shop, can hardly be considered part of *Pygmalion*. Written for the play's first edition in 1916, it was Shaw's first major volley at romantics who palpitated for a Cinderella ending. Most audiences will not know of it. The play must stand on its own without it.

Still, those who have closely observed a good performance of *Pygmalion* can realize how consistently most of the afterword evolves from the play's characters and action. The greatest exception is Clara, whom the afterword reclaims beyond the pathetic snob we have seen. The space devoted to her change for the better may seem lengthy for so minor a character unless we recall how Eliza's despair over social isolation in act 4 resembles Clara's plight in acts 1 and 3. Each responds to the problem quite differently, however. Clara plays up to Higgins as a matrimonial prospect in act 3, yet when he later suggests that his mother might arrange a prospect for Eliza, the former flower girl replies, "We were above that at the corner of Tottenham Court Road. . . . I sold flowers. I didnt sell myself" (102–3). She has more integrity and intrinsic "class" than Clara.

The End

Eliza's acute sensitivity reiterates a theme more persistent than phonetics throughout the play. Besides pretensions of birthright, which no one earns, what makes a lady? Education. Training. A genteel lifestyle. And what provides these? Money, or marriage to a gentleman. For phonetics lessons and beautiful dresses, Eliza needs money, which Pickering provides; in the afterword, he also funds Eliza and Freddy's business enterprise, while Clara learns how to earn money and maintain self-respect at the same time.

What about the romance of marriage then? At the start of the afterword, Shaw divorces *Pygmalion*'s outcome from unimaginative marital happy endings by stressing another type of romance: "Now, the history of Eliza Doolittle, though called a romance because the transfiguration it records seems exceedingly improbable, is common enough. Such transfigurations have been achieved by hundreds of resolutely ambitious young women since Nell Gwynne" (134). Like Nell and others, Eliza rises socially through the rigorous efforts her ambition requires. Such transformations may be "common enough," yet transformations of all sorts have universal appeal. Ovid depicts hundreds in his *Metamorphoses*; Cinderella's is central to the world's most popular fairy tale; and Shaw deploys chords from both. At the same time, however, his *Pygmalion* has unique tonality as it counterpoints those chords with contemporary realism. Cinderella ascends on her godmother's magic, an external force. Pygmalion's statue breathes because his prayer is answered by Venus, an external force. Higgins's phonetics magic and Eliza's affection for him echo these, but more important are Eliza's talents and her resolute ambition—internal, very human energy.

By the time Eliza uses this energy to hurl Higgins's slippers at him, and Higgins—after praying, not to Venus but, "Thank God it's all over"—suggests that she marry someone else, Perrault's "Cinderella" and Ovid's "Pygmalion" have become foils for the action more than complements to it. And as though to have his cake and eat it several times over, Shaw then inserts another shift, a grotesquerie that satirizes the fairy tale and the myth. Nearer to their magical mode than Eliza is Doolittle, who blossoms as the play's ultimate Cinderella: after a life of collecting garbage and avoiding work, he suddenly finds himself wealthy and, resplendently transmogrified, goes off to his wedding. Doolittle's dismay at this dazzling fate is an ultimate joke: Cinderella's delight is a sensible man's blight.

The step-by-step growth in Eliza, which coheres the play when its romantic mythical associations are fracturing, contrasts with Higgins's temperamental swings from one moment to the next. It would seem that little coheres these other than pride, professional dedication, and devil imagery. Does the devil imagery have a function besides its color and humor? Shaw's final observation in the afterword offers a hint as it presents a sly perspective on Eliza's ambivalence toward Higgins: "She has even secret mischievous moments in which she wishes she could get him alone, on a desert island . . . and just drag him off his pedestal and see him making love like any common man. . . . But when it comes to business, to the life that she really leads as distinguished from the life of dreams and fancies, she likes Freddy and she likes the Colonel; and she does not like Higgins and Mr Doolittle. Galatea never does quite like Pygmalion: his relation to her is too godlike to be altogether agreeable" (148).

Godlike? How does this jibe with her "Oh, you *are* a devil" in act 5? *Pygmalion* could be perceived as a type of morality play (a dramatized moral allegory), with Higgins holding a diabolical tuning fork. In act 1 Eliza evokes shades of an unrealized Eve, a "good girl" among squashed cabbage leaves in the Covent Garden produce market— London's version of a fruitful Garden of Eden—where she is attended by divine omens in thunder and lightning and the striking of St. Paul's clock. In act 2 this latter-day Eve is tempted by a proud devil with a goody from a dessert dish filled with fruit. She succumbs to the temptation of his tree of knowledge and takes phonetic lessons, a decision she regrets when the Paradise of Mrs. Higgins's flat (in which the devil gloats over her soul) and of the embassy reception in act 3 leads to a hell of lonely self-knowledge in act 4, where the callous devil munches an apple from the dessert dish of her fall. By act 5, increasingly grasping self-knowledge and wending between earthly alternatives, she boldly calls him a devil. He appears to embody the worst demon of all: a haughtily presumptuous, God-mimicking, Miltonic one. Now this devil wants her to put up with his abuse forever, but she foils him at

last, saving her soul by declaring her independence and joining a loving savior, Freddy, with whom she had collided, under omens of heavenly lightning, in act 1.

Against such a tidy view, however, we can also see the development of a transcendent ambiguity in Higgins. Images of him as a
tempter or brute occur largely in acts 2 and 4. He is driven by pride
and his profession in each case, but factors in both acts contribute to
Eliza's evolution. Enclosing these acts, utterances about Eliza's soul,
all from Higgins, emerge strategically in acts 1, 3, and 5, and all recognize the significance of, or aim at, the growth of her soul. Act 5, in
which Eliza calls him both a devil and a preacher, is most ambiguous
when Higgins translates his affection for her into an affection for all
humanity.

In toto, Higgins, more obsessed or playful than evil, offers Eliza
a means to illumination and salvation, a means to articulate the divinity within her, and he forwards these ends, convinced of their value for
all humanity.

Such convictions call forth yet another myth that Shaw knew
well, that of Prometheus, one of the demigodly Titans who ruled the
world before the Greek gods superseded them. Taking pity on
humankind when Zeus contemplated destroying it, Prometheus stole
fire from the gods and brought it to earth for humanity's survival and
illumination. Thus, to ancient Greeks, Prometheus was a benefactor
and culture hero, one with qualities that Higgins represents in his references to heaven, to "my own spark of divine fire," and in his declaration, "I care for life, for humanity" (126–27). Yet there is a
paradoxical rub to the myth of Prometheus. Its gist also suggests that,
centuries after its Greek origins, early Christians reinterpreted it, converting Prometheus, his fire, and his rebellion against Zeus into the
devil rebelling against God and tempting humankind with fruit from
the tree of knowledge. With lively metaphoric crosscurrents, therefore,
it appears that Higgins partakes of the myth's doubleness as part
tempter and part savior—metaphysical extensions of other extremes in
his personality.

Such extremes confound Eliza. Little wonder she would like to
drag the professor off his pedestal and see him making love like any

common man. Ovid often allures readers with tales of gods who assumed human or animal shapes to make love to humans. But what Eliza has learned through her experience with Higgins makes such fancies incidental. She has learned to express her inner strength, and this strength may well tell her that life with him would involve either repeated battles or her subservience. Higgins demonstrates the good sense of her leaving him at the end of the play when, just after he has extolled her independence, he once again calls her "you little fool" and orders her (despite his admiration of her independence moments before) to fetch and carry for him (like a servant or puppy). A motor bus over twice one's age, with a Miltonic mind, a god complex, and a mother complex may be fun until it runs over you twice a week. If it must be married, marry it to someone you dislike. Or leave it a bachelor.

For Eliza's sake, Shaw offers Freddy as a compensation: good-looking, kindly, well-mannered, loving, near her age, not too smart but ready, willing, and amiable. Of course, Higgins is more intelligent and could be more exciting, if one does not mind being run over. Meanwhile, Shaw shows how relative and varied intelligence may be: apart from Clara, women in the play, even Doolittle's mistress, appear wiser than the men. Today, Mrs. Higgins and Mrs. Eynsford Hill are, alas, largely out of date. In sophistication, Eliza may be somewhere between the two but, at the very least, her native intelligence rivals that of both, and she has an advantage they do not: she can work. She can in fact be "a lady in a flower shop" in a union with Freddy that joins her strength with his weakness, her lower-class background with his genteel one, not only a happy union but also a symbolic one that epitomizes the forthcoming, more egalitarian social order. In comparison to Shaw's Eliza, the slave who returns to Higgins at the end of the film version and *My Fair Lady* is in fact a fool. One is a modern spirit, the other is mid-Victorian.

In sum, as Eliza's social parable of success demonstrates "the movement of consciousness from lower to higher levels of reality, the steady remaking of character," it has spiritual overtones of—and connects, modestly, to—phases in Underhill's composite portrait of mystics. These phases finally arrive at "(5) *Union*: the true goal of the mystic quest. In this state the Absolute Life is not merely perceived and

enjoyed by the Self, as in Illumination: but is *one* with it. This is the end towards which all the previous oscillations of consciousness have tended. It is a state of equilibrium, of purely spiritual life; characterized by peaceful joy, by enhanced powers, by intense certitude."

Having realized the falseness of her success and her social isolation after the embassy reception, Eliza finds her place in Mrs. Higgins's drawing room where, very much at home, she might almost be the lady's daughter. Now she can play with her old role ironically, mock Higgins cunningly, articulate what she feels better than he can, and assert her independence. In short, she is now "*one*" with this environment, showing "enhanced powers." Her declaration of independence reveals "intense certitude," whereupon she achieves "a state of equilibrium" in bidding Higgins goodbye, and if Shaw may be allowed to have his way, she is looking forward to "peaceful joy" with Freddy, something she could never have achieved with the professor. She has her own soul now, chastened and wiser. Intrinsically and ultimately self-created, she experiences an enlightened sense of belonging, of union.

The world, of course, particularly Shaw's world, does not end with welling music. He is too aware of anticlimax, of continuing struggles, and of the need for struggles both mundane and spiritual in human evolution. Yet the struggles inherent to Eliza's growth are life-affirming, a deeply grounded affirmation that, along with the play's life-affirming mythical echoes, gives *Pygmalion* particular resonance and fun as comedy.

Though it seems destined that fewer persons will recognize Eliza Doolittle than Cinderella, it also appears that more know about Higgins and Eliza than about Pygmalion and Galatea. Thus, *Pygmalion*, revitalizing ancient myths as did Perrault's "Cinderella" and Ovid's "Pygmalion," has entered the mythical pantheon. But to give the myth a Shavian twist, we may allow Eliza to realize herself in a union with society and Freddy, not Higgins. Inverting an old adage, à la Shaw, she probably understands that it is better to be a young man's sweetheart than an old man's slave.

Notes and References

Chapter 1

1. For autobiographical backgrounds, see the preface to *Immaturity* in *The Works of Bernard Shaw*, vol. 1 (London: Constable & Co., 1930); *Sixteen Self Sketches* (London: Constable & Co., 1949); Stanley Weintraub, *Shaw: An Autobiography 1856–1898* (New York: Weybright and Talley, 1969).

2. For backgrounds and good translations of the myth, see Mary M. Innes, *The* Metamorphoses *of Ovid* (Baltimore: Penguin Books); and A. D. Melville and E. J. Kenny, *Ovid:* Metamorphoses (Oxford: Oxford University Press, 1986).

3. See *The Fairy Tales of Charles Perrault*, translated and introduced by Geoffrey Brereton (Baltimore: Penguin Books, 1957).

Chapter 2

1. For example, see "The Sanity of Art" in *The Works of Bernard Shaw* (London: Constable & Co., 1931), 19:328–29.

2. La Scala Autographs, Catalog 62 (March 1991), 7.

Chapter 3

1. Christopher St. John, ed., *Ellen Terry and Bernard Shaw: A Correspondence* (New York: Putnam's Sons, 1932), 186.

2. Ibid., 326.

3. See Alan Dent, ed., *Bernard Shaw and Mrs. Patrick Campbell: Their Correspondence* (London: Victor Gollancz, 1952).

4. Quoted in Rodelle Weintraub, ed., *Fabian Feminist* (University Park: Pennsylvania State University Press, 1977), 39.

5. See Richard Hugget, *The Truth about* Pygmalion (London: William Heinemann, 1969), 141–55.

6. Ibid., endpaper, and 145–56.

7. Ibid., endpaper.

8. H. W. Massingham, *Nation* (18 April 1914); reprinted in T. F. Evans, ed., *Shaw: The Critical Heritage* (London: Routledge & Kegan Paul, 1976), 226–29.

9. Desmond MacCarthy, (18 April 1914); reprinted in his *Shaw: The Plays* (1951; reprint, Newton Abbot, Eng.: David & Charles, 1973), 108–11.

10. The fullest articles on Dickens as a source are Michael Goldberg, "Shaw's *Pygmalion*: The Reworking of *Great Expectations*," *Shaw Review* 22 (1979): 14–22; and Martin Quinn, "The Informing Presence of Charles Dickens in Bernard Shaw's *Pygmalion*," *Dickensian* 80 (1984): 144–50.

11. On Bacon, see Thomas Kranidas, "Sir Francis Bacon and Shaw's *Pygmalion*," *Shaw Review* 9 (1967): 77; on Gilbert's *Pygmalion and Galatea* (and others), see Errol Durbach, "Pygmalion: Myth and Anti-Myth in the Plays of Ibsen and Shaw," *English Studies in Africa* 21 (1978): 23–31, and Jane M. Miller "Some Versions of Pygmalion," in *Ovidian Influences on Literature and Art*, edited by Charles Martindale (Cambridge: Cambridge University Press, 1988), 205–14; on *A Doll's House*, see Norbert F. O'Donnell, "On the 'Unpleasantness' of *Pygmalion*," *Shaw Bulletin* 1, no. 2 (1955): 8, and Bernard F. Dukore, *Bernard Shaw, Playwright: Aspects of Shavian Drama* (Columbia: University of Missouri Press, 1973), 60–64, and Maurice Valency, *The Cart and the Trumpet: The Plays of George Bernard Shaw* (New York: Oxford University Press, 1973), 314; on Ibsen's *When We Dead Awaken*, see Richard Burton, *Bernard Shaw: The Man and the Mask* (New York: Henry Holt and Co., 1916), 181, and Valency, *The Cart and the Trumpet*, 319, and Durbach, "Pygmalion: Myth and Anti-Myth," 26–27; on other possibilities, see E. F. Briden, "James's Miss Chum: Another of Eliza's Prototypes?" *Shaw Review* 19 (1976): 17–22, and Sara Moore Putzell, "Another Source for *Pygmalion*: G.B.S. and M. E. Braddon," *Shaw Review* 22 (1979): 29–32.

12. Quoted in Archibald Henderson, *George Bernard Shaw: Man of the Century* (New York: Appleton-Century-Crofts, 1956), 614.

13. Ibid., 616.

14. See Bernard F. Dukore, *The Collected Screenplays of Bernard Shaw* (Athens: University of Georgia Press, 1980), 40–49, 63–87.

15. Dan H. Laurence, ed., *Bernard Shaw: Collected Letters 1926–1950* (New York: Viking, 1988), 815.

16. William Irvine, *The Universe of G.B.S.* (New York: Whittlesey House, 1949), 289; Milton Crane, "*Pygmalion*: Bernard Shaw's Dramatic Theory and Practice," *PMLA* 66 (December 1951): 879–85; St. John Ervine, *Bernard Shaw: His Life, Work and Friends* (London: Constable & Co., 1956),

460; Alan Jay Lerner, "*Pygmalion* and *My Fair Lady*," *Shaw Bulletin* 1, no. 10 (1956): 7; Valency, *The Cart and the Trumpet*, 314–15.

17. Eric Bentley, *Bernard Shaw 1856–1950* (New York: New Directions, 1957), 122–23.

18. See O'Donnell, "On the 'Unpleasantness,'" 7–10; Dukore, *Bernard Shaw, Playwright*, 61; Durbach, "Pygmalion: Myth and Anti-Myth," 30–31.

19. Peter Ure, "Master and Pupil in Bernard Shaw," *Essays in Criticism* 19 (1969): 119–39; and Lisë Pedersen, "Shakespeare's *The Taming of the Shrew* vs. Shaw's *Pygmalion*: Male Chauvinism vs. Women's Lib?" in Weintraub, *Fabian Feminist*, 14–22.

20. Myron Matlaw, "The Dénouement of *Pygmalion*," *Modern Drama* 1 (1958): 29–34; Stanley J. Solomon, "The Ending of *Pygmalion*: A Structural View," *Educational Theatre Journal* 16 (1964): 59–63; Louis Crompton, *Shaw the Dramatist* (Lincoln: University of Nebraska Press, 1969), 146–51.

21. J. L. Wisenthal, *The Marriage of Contraries: Bernard Shaw's Middle Plays* (Cambridge, Mass.: Harvard University Press, 1974), 123–25.

22. Martin Meisel, *Shaw and the Nineteenth-Century Theater* (Princeton, N.J.: Princeton University Press, 1963), 176–77; Diderik Roll-Hansen, "Shaw's *Pygmalion*: The Two Versions of 1916 and 1941," *Review of English Literature* 8, no. 4 (1967): 81–90.

23. A striking exception is Timothy G. Vesonder, who applies the mythical transformation aspect of Pygmalion and Cinderella to Eliza's spiritual change at the play's end. See "Eliza's Choice: Transformation Myth and the Ending of *Pygmalion*," in Weintraub, *Fabian Feminist*, 43–44.

24. Massingham, 227–28; Bentley, *Bernard Shaw*, 121. Miller finds a link (anticipating Shaw?) between a Christian reinterpretation of Ovid's "Pygmalion" and a Cinderella motif in a fourteenth-century French poem, "Ovide moralisé," 208.

25. See Bertrand M. Wainger, "Henry Sweet—Shaw's *Pygmalion*," *Studies in Philology* 27 (1930): 558–72; Abraham Tauber, ed., *Bernard Shaw on Language* (New York: Philosophical Library, 1963); Lawrence Langner, *G.B.S. and the Lunatic* (New York: Atheneum, 1963), 258–71; Michael Holroyd, *Bernard Shaw*, vol. 2 (New York: Random House, 1989), 325–26.

26. MacCarthy, 112.

27. See Arnold Silver, *Bernard Shaw: The Darker Side* (Stanford, Calif.: Stanford University Press, 1982), 179–250, 253–79; and Holroyd, *Bernard Shaw*, 2:328–30. Silver devotes over 100 pages to *Pygmalion*, but his unbalanced pursuit of Shaw's "darker side" often causes his Freudian hat to fall over his eyes.

28. See *Collected Letters*, 3:13–19; *Sixteen Self Sketches*, 113.

Chapter 5

1. Observant readers of the Penguin edition may notice that the etching at the head of act 2 does not match this description. Either the artist or an editor failed to read Shaw's play, because the etching is of Mrs. Higgins's drawing room (see acts 3 and 5), which has three large windows. But even for that setting, the artist has misplaced Mrs. Higgins's desk and other furniture. Such confusion helps explain why Shaw often directed his plays and provided careful descriptions (for those who could read). Penguin Books should correct the problem.

2. See "Laughter" by Henri Bergson, and "An Essay on Comedy" by George Meredith; both in *Comedy*, edited by Wylie Sypher (Garden City, N.Y.: Doubleday & Co., 1956).

3. Bernard Shaw, *Major Barbara* (New York: Viking Penguin, n.d.), 17.

4. See Shaw's preface to *The Shewing-up of Blanco Posnet*, in *The Works of Bernard Shaw* (London: Constable & Co., 1930), 12:380–81.

Chapter 6

1. Readers may notice how inadequately the etchings on these pages represent Mrs. Higgins and her drawing room.

2. *Pygmalion* and *My Fair Lady* (New York: Signet/New American Library, 1975), 152.

Chapter 7

1. Yet another choice was made by directors of the film, in which Eliza tenderly replaces the ring on her finger. And another exists in a longhand scenario by Shaw: "She finds it, holds it in triumph, and replaces it on her finger" (British Library ms. 171; cited by Roll-Hansen, "Shaw's *Pygmalion*: The Two Versions," 89n). So directors have tantalizing possibilities.

2. Delivered on 21 March 1912; reprinted in *The Religious Speeches of Bernard Shaw*, edited by Warren S. Smith (University Park: Pennsylvania State University Press, 1963), 38, 48.

3. *Religious Speeches*, 33.

4. Evelyn Underhill, *Mysticism* (reprint, New York: Doubleday, 1990), 168–70.

Chapter 8

1. See *Paradise Lost*, book 1, line 26; and Blake's *The Marriage of Heaven and Hell*, plate 5n.

2. See Dukore, *Collected Screenplays*, 272.

Selected Bibliography

Primary Sources

The Works of Bernard Shaw. Standard Edition. 37 vols. London: Constable & Co., 1930–50.

Ellen Terry and Bernard Shaw: A Correspondence. Edited by Christopher St. John. New York: G. P. Putnam's Sons, 1932.

Sixteen Self Sketches. London: Constable & Co., 1949.

Bernard Shaw and Mrs. Patrick Campbell: Their Correspondence. Edited by Alan Dent. London: Victor Gollancz, 1952.

Shaw on Theatre. Edited by E. J. West. New York: Hill and Wang, 1958.

To a Young Actress: The Letters of Bernard Shaw to Molly Tompkins. Edited by Peter Tompkins. New York: Clarkson N. Potter, 1960.

Bernard Shaw on Language. Edited by Abraham Tauber. New York: Philosophical Library, 1963.

The Religious Speeches of Bernard Shaw. Edited by Warren S. Smith. University Park: Pennsylvania State University Press, 1963.

Bernard Shaw: Collected Letters 1874–1897; 1898–1910. 2 vols. Edited by Dan H. Laurence. New York: Dodd, Mead & Co., 1963, 1972.

Shaw: An Autobiography 1856–1898. Selected from his writings by Stanley Weintraub. New York: Weybright and Talley, 1969.

Shaw: An Autobiography 1898–1950: The Playwright Years. Selected from his writings by Stanley Weintraub. New York: Weybright and Talley, 1970.

The Bodley Head Bernard Shaw: Collected Plays with their Prefaces. 7 vols. Edited by Dan H. Laurence. London: Max Reinhardt, 1970–74.

The Collected Screenplays of Bernard Shaw. Edited by Bernard F. Dukore. Athens: University of Georgia Press, 1980.

Bernard Shaw: Agitations: Letters to the Press 1875–1950. Edited by Dan H. Laurence and James Rambeau. New York: Frederick Ungar Publishing Co., 1985.

Bernard Shaw: Collected Letters 1911–1925, 1926–1950. 2 vols. Edited by Dan H. Laurence. New York: Viking, 1985, 1988.

Secondary Sources

Bibliographies and Reference Works

Bevan, Dean. *A Concordance to the Plays and Prefaces of Bernard Shaw*. 10 vols. Detroit: Gale Research, 1971. An early example of computer-driven concordances. Entries set briefly in context. Useful for names, topics, themes, or for locating certain passages.

Laurence, Dan H. *Bernard Shaw: A Bibliography*. 2 vols. Oxford: Clarendon Press, 1983. Meticulous, detailed, very thorough.

Wearing, J. P., et al. *G. B. Shaw: An Annotated Bibliography of Writings about Him*. Vol. 1: 1871–1930, compiled by J. P. Wearing; vol. 2: 1931–1956, compiled by Elsie B. Adams and Donald C. Haberman; vol. 3: 1957–1978, compiled by Donald C. Haberman. Dekalb: Northern Illinois University Press, 1986, 1987. An impossibly immense international job that called for selectivity, but as well done as anyone is likely to do in the near future.

Biographies

Ervine, St. John. *Bernard Shaw: His Life, Work and Friends*. London: Constable & Co., 1956. By one of Shaw's friends, a former actor. Opinionated, not profound.

Henderson, Archibald. *George Bernard Shaw: Man of the Century*. New York: Appleton-Century-Crofts, 1956. Shaw designated Henderson his "authorized" biographer, giving him much material. This work revises and updates Henderson's *George Bernard Shaw: His Life and Works* (1911) and *Bernard Shaw: Playboy and Prophet* (1932), which contain good caricatures and photographs of Shaw and other worthwhile details not in *Man of the Century*.

Holroyd, Michael. *Bernard Shaw*. Vol. 1: 1856–1898; vol. 2: 1898–1920; vol. 3: 1920–1950. New York: Random House, 1988, 1989, 1991.

The most recent, most comprehensive biography. Well-written; especially good on Shaw's friendships and backgrounds; less insightful on Shaw's plays. Volume 3 is best; the first two are often derivative from others' works.

Hugget, Richard. *The Truth about "Pygmalion."* London: William Heinemann, 1969. Recounts the background of the writing of the play, Shaw's relations with Mrs. Patrick Campbell and Beerbohm Tree regarding it, its rehearsals, and its sensational opening night.

Irvine, William. *The Universe of G.B.S.* New York: Whittlesey House, 1949. Interesting biographically and for comments on Shaw's plays.

Pearson, Hesketh. *George Bernard Shaw: His Life and Personality.* New York: Atheneum, 1963. Updates his *G.B.S.: A Full Length Portrait* (1942). Particularly valuable because Shaw edited and added much to it.

Peters, Margot. *Bernard Shaw and the Actresses.* Garden City, N.Y.: Doubleday, 1980. Shaw's relations with many women. Finely written; a source of much in Holroyd's first volume.

Weintraub, Rodelle, ed. *Shaw Abroad.* University Park: Pennsylvania State University Press, 1985. Essays on Shaw's travels.

Weintraub, Stanley. *Journey to Heartbreak: The Crucible Years of Bernard Shaw 1914–1918.* New York: Weybright and Talley, 1971. An excellent account of Shaw's World War I activities.

Critical Studies: Books

Bentley, Eric. *Bernard Shaw 1856–1950.* Amended Edition. New York: New Directions, 1957. The best short study of Shaw's political and artistic temperament and his plays.

Berst, Charles A. *Bernard Shaw and the Art of Drama.* Urbana: University of Illinois Press, 1973. Analyzes the aesthetics of ten of Shaw's major plays, including *Pygmalion*.

Bertolini, John A. *The Playwrighting Self of Bernard Shaw.* Carbondale: Southern Illinois University Press, 1991. Includes an interesting psychological view of Shaw in relation to *Pygmalion*.

Bloom, Harold, ed. *Modern Critical Views: George Bernard Shaw.* New York: Chelsea House, 1987. Reprints critical essays and chapters on Shaw. Bloom has also edited a similar volume on *Pygmalion* (1988).

Burton, Richard. *Bernard Shaw: The Man and the Mask.* New York: Henry Holt and Co., 1916. A good early view of Shaw and his plays, including *Pygmalion*.

Carpenter, Charles A. *Bernard Shaw & the Art of Destroying Ideals: The Early Plays.* Madison: University of Wisconsin Press, 1969. An effective study of Shaw's iconoclastic art. Does not include *Pygmalion*.

Chesterton, G. K. *George Bernard Shaw*. London: John Lane, 1909. A fine early appraisal of Shaw by a renowned contemporary.

Costello, Donald P. *The Serpent's Eye: Shaw and the Cinema*. Notre Dame, Ind.: University of Notre Dame Press, 1965. Has a good chapter that relates the film to the play.

Crompton, Louis. *Shaw the Dramatist*. Lincoln: University of Nebraska Press, 1969. A sensitive analysis of Shaw's dramas, including an excellent chapter on *Pygmalion*.

Dukore, Bernard F. *Bernard Shaw, Playwright: Aspects of Shavian Drama*. Columbia: University of Missouri Press, 1973. A perceptive study, with an emphasis on the social aspects of *Pygmalion*.

Evans, T. F., ed. *Shaw: The Critical Heritage*. London: Routledge & Kegan Paul, 1976. A useful and enlightening anthology of contemporary critical responses to Shaw, concentrating on his plays.

Gordon, David J. *Bernard Shaw and the Comic Sublime*. New York: Macmillan, 1990. A theoretical view of Shaw's comedy, stressing its seriousness.

Kronenberger, Louis, ed. *George Bernard Shaw: A Critical Survey*. Cleveland: World Publishing Co., 1953. Includes critiques of Shaw and his drama by notable contemporaries.

MacCarthy, Desmond. *Shaw: The Plays*. 1951; reprint, Newton Abbot, Eng.: David & Charles, 1973. Collects MacCarthy's reviews of 27 Shaw plays, including *Pygmalion* as a play and a film. Urbane, brilliant.

Meisel, Martin. *Shaw and the Nineteenth-Century Theater*. Princeton, N.J.: Princeton University Press, 1963. A highly informed study of the influence of Victorian theater on Shaw's plays, with short but good analyses of the plays.

Morgan, Margery M. *The Shavian Playground: An Exploration of the Art of George Bernard Shaw*. London: Methuen & Co., 1972. Offers stimulating perspectives on Shavian drama but little on *Pygmalion*.

Ohmann, Richard M. *Shaw: The Style and the Man*. Middletown, Conn.: Wesleyan University Press, 1962. A good analysis of Shaw's style.

Silver, Arnold. *Bernard Shaw: The Darker Side*. Stanford, Calif.: Stanford University Press, 1982. An unbalanced work that includes *Pygmalion* but takes psychological nose dives.

Turco, Alfred, Jr. *Shaw's Moral Vision: The Self and Salvation*. Ithaca, N.Y.: Cornell University Press, 1976. A thoughtful study of Shaw's philosophical and spiritual side.

Valency, Maurice. *The Cart and the Trumpet: The Plays of George Bernard Shaw*. New York: Oxford University Press, 1973. This should have been much better than it is. It places Shaw in dramatic contexts but is seldom penetrating about his plays.

Whitman, Robert F. *Shaw and the Play of Ideas.* Ithaca, N.Y.: Cornell University Press, 1977. A fine complement to Turco's book.

Wisenthal, J. L. *The Marriage of Contraries: Bernard Shaw's Middle Plays.* Cambridge, Mass.: Harvard University Press, 1974. A bright, stimulating work that finds Higgins creating the lady in Eliza and she creating the woman.

Critical Studies: Articles

Crane, Milton. "*Pygmalion*: Bernard Shaw's Dramatic Theory and Practice." *PMLA* 66 (December 1951): 879–85. Finds the play more a classical comedy than a Shavian discussion play.

Dukore, Bernard F. "'The Middleaged Bully and the Girl of Eighteen': The Ending They *Didn't* Film." *Shaw Review* 14 (1971): 102–6. This found its way into Dukore's edition of Shaw's screenplays (1980), which should be consulted for his fine 153-page introduction.

Matlaw, Myron. "The Dénouement of *Pygmalion*." *Modern Drama* 1 (1958): 29–34. Compares Higgins with Pygmalion as a giver of life, versus the Higgins of *My Fair Lady*.

O'Donnell, Norbert F. "On the 'Unpleasantness' of *Pygmalion*." *Shaw Bulletin* 1, no. 2 (1955): 7–10. Compares Eliza's growth to independence with Ibsen's *A Doll's House*.

Pedersen, Lisë. "Shakespeare's *The Taming of the Shrew* vs. Shaw's *Pygmalion*: Male Chauvinism vs. Women's Lib?" In *Fabian Feminist*, edited by Rodelle Weintraub, 14–22. University Park: Pennsylvania State University Press, 1977. Pits Shaw's feminist view of a woman's metamorphosis against Shakespeare's male chauvinist view.

Roll-Hansen, Diderik. "Shaw's *Pygmalion*: The Two Versions of 1916 and 1941." *Review of English Literature* 8, no. 4 (1967): 81–90. Offers evidence from British Museum manuscripts and prefers the "subtle ambivalence" of the original endings to acts 4 and 5 over Shaw's later revisions of them.

Solomon, Stanley J. "The Ending of *Pygmalion*: A Structural View." *Educational Theatre Journal* 16 (1964): 59–63. Higgins creates a new human being whose independence of him is crucial to the play's ending.

Ure, Peter. "Master and Pupil in Bernard Shaw." *Essays in Criticism* 19 (1969): 119–39. Finds a reversal of Shaw's usual pattern: in *Pygmalion*, Eliza is independent from the start, and Higgins, the educator, is educated by the end.

Vesonder, Timothy G. "Eliza's Choice: Transformation Myth and the Ending of *Pygmalion*." In *Fabian Feminist*, edited by Rodelle Weintraub, 39–45. University Park: Pennsylvania State University Press, 1977. *Pygmalion* reflects transformation myths, not popular romance: a Higgins-Eliza marriage would elevate him and reduce her.

Index

Clothing, as representative of class:
of Doolittle, 118; of Eliza, 33,
36, 70, 71, 78, 92, 93, 104,
114, 124; of the Eynsford
Hills, 30, 33; of Higgins 36;
of Mrs. Higgins, 75
Comedy: of character (*see* Doolittle,
Alfred; Eliza, attributes of;
Eliza, dehumanization of;
Higgins, Henry; Meredith,
George); of contrasts, dislocations, incongruities, inversions,
shifts, twists, 53–58, 64–70,
78–82; of humans as machinelike (*see* Bergson, Henri); of
manners, 76–81, 121–26
Cornwallis-West, George, an aristocratic version of Freddy, 17
Crompton, Louis, 23

Darwin, Charles: *Origin of Species*,
3; *Descent of Man*, 3
DeMille, Cecil B., 93
Devil: Higgins as, 54, 59–60, 83, 85,
88, 96, 103, 104, 127, 132,
138; Higgins as a Miltonic
type of, 129–30, 138; in
Pygmalion, 5, 13; in Shaw's
mien, 5
Dickens, Charles, as a source of
characters and incidents in
Pygmalion, 20
Directors and actors: need to orchestrate duet of Higgins and
Pickering, 90; Shaw's cues to,
33, 45, 50–52, 105–8
Doolittle, Alfred, 64–70, 117–21. *See
also*, Morality, Middle-class
Dramatic economy, 34, 80–81, 126;
of minor characters playing
major roles, 31, 92

Edward VII, 95
Einstein, Albert, 29–30

Eliza, ATTRIBUTES OF: affectionate,
120, 128–31, 133; a colorful
storyteller, 82; good-humored,
43, 106–7; ingenious, 124;
inwardly strong, 140; a linguistic and musical genius,
90–91; morally sensitive,
33–34, 42, 103–4; practical,
intelligent, farsighted, 55–56,
101; rhetorically skilled, 101,
103–4, 131; sensitively ironic,
101, 122; sharp-eared and a
quick learner, 42–43, 57–58,
101; socially and spiritually
well-balanced, 141; sophisticated, 121–124, 128, 140–41;
talented and tenacious, 34–35,
60, 105–6, 132–33, 137. *See
also* Cinderella fairy tale;
Comedy; Doolittle, Alfred;
Eve, Eliza as; Feelings; Film
scenes; Higgins, Mrs.; Life
force spirit, Eliza's; Marriage;
Money; Pearce, Mrs.; Poverty;
Prostitution; *Pygmalion*; Role
playing; Taxis.
DEHUMANIZATION OF: by
animal fear, 54; by her howls,
42, 86–87, 100, 125, 131; by
Higgins treating her as an animal, object, subject, 52,
57–58, 63, 72, 100–101, 116,
122–23; as a lost soul, 53–54;
by her snobbery, 70–71, 80,
89–90, 125–26.
TRANSFORMATION OF: in
her awakening, 29, 43, 88,
110–13; in her dark night of
the soul, 110–13; in her illumination, 78–80, 89, 95,
110–13; in her purgation, 56,
62–63, 72, 89, 110–13; and
union with genteel society,
121–24, 140–41

Index

Index

The Author

Charles Berst is a professor of English at the University of California at Los Angeles, where he has taught modern drama and English literature for 27 years. His publications include *Bernard Shaw and the Art of Drama* (1973), numerous articles on Shaw's life and plays, and an edited collection of essays, *Shaw and Religion* (1980). He serves on the editorial board of *SHAW: The Annual of Bernard Shaw Studies* and is currently writing a book on Shaw's late-life affair with an amorous young American, Molly Tomkins. At UCLA, he has received a Distinguished Teaching Award and a University Service Award, and has served as chair of the College of Letters and Science faculty, and chair of the faculty senate.